Workbook

WORLD ENGLISH 1

THIRD EDITION

Real People • Real Places • Real Language

Workbook

WORLD ENGLISH 1

THIRD EDITION

Real People • Real Places • Real Language

NATIONAL GEOGRAPHIC
LEARNING

Australia • Brazil • Mexico • Singapore • United Kingdom • United States

NATIONAL GEOGRAPHIC
LEARNING

National Geographic Learning,
a Cengage Company

***World English Level 1 Workbook: Real People, Real Places, Real Language*, Third Edition**

Publisher: Sherrise Roehr
Executive Editor: Sarah Kenney
Development Editor: Adam Robinson
Media Researcher: Leila Hishmeh
Director of Global Marketing: Ian Martin
Senior Product Marketing Manager: Caitlin Thomas
Heads of Regional Marketing:
Charlotte Ellis (Europe, Middle East, and Africa)
Kiel Hamm (Asia) Irina Pereyra (Latin America)
Production Manager: Daisy Sosa
Manufacturing Planner: Mary Beth Hennebury
Art Director: Brenda Carmichael
Operations Support: Hayley Chwazik-Gee
Cover Image: Trey Ratcliff
Compositor: MPS Limited

World English 1 Workbook ISBN: 978-0-357-11371-4

National Geographic Learning
200 Pier 4 Boulevard
Boston, MA 02210
USA

Locate your local office at **international.cengage.com/region**

Visit National Geographic Learning online at **ELTNGL.com**

Visit our corporate website at www.cengage.com

Printed in China
Print Number: 02 Print Year: 2023

Contents

Student book scope and sequence

Unit	Unit Goals	Grammar	Vocabulary
1 People Page 2 	• Meet People • Ask for Personal Information • Describe People and Occupations • Compare People's Jobs • Write a Personal Description	Review of Simple Present *Be* *Wh-* Questions with *Be* *Be* + Adjective (+ Noun)	Occupations Countries Nationalities Descriptive Adjectives
2 A Day in the Life Page 16 	• Talk about a Typical Day • Talk about Free Time • Describe a Special Day • Talk about Hobbies and Interests • Plan a Party	Review of Simple Present Prepositions of Time Adverbs of Frequency	Daily Activities Party Words Celebrations and Festivals
3 Going Places Page 30 	• Talk about Your Possessions • Ask for and Give Travel Information • Ask for and Give Advice • Plan a Vacation • Describe a Place	Possession Possessive Adjectives and Pronouns *Belong to* Imperatives and *should* for Advice	Travel Preparation and Stages Travel Documents Describing Places
4 Food Page 44 	• Describe a Recipe • Order a Meal • Talk about Diets • Plan a Farm or Garden • Follow and Give Instructions	Count and Non-count Nouns: *a / an, some,* and *any* *How much* and *How many* with quantifiers: *lots of / a lot of, a few, a little, not many, not much*	Food Food Groups Diets
5 Sports Page 58 	• Describe Activities Happening Now • Compare Everyday and Present-Time Activities • Talk about Your Favorite Sports • Compare Sports and Activities • Write and Complete a Questionnaire	Present Continuous Simple Present and Present Continuous Stative Verbs	Doing Sports Present-Time Activities Team and Individual Sports
6 Destinations Page 72 	• Discuss Past Vacations • Ask about a Trip • Talk about Your Weekend • Describe an Ancient Place • Find and Share Information Online	Simple Past Regular and Irregular Verbs Simple Past of *to be*	Travel Activities Emphatic Adjectives

Listening	Speaking and Pronunciation	Reading	Writing	Video Journal
Focused Listening: Personal Introductions	Asking For and Giving Personal Information Starting a Conversation Contractions of *be* Word Stress	The Best Job in the World	Writing descriptions of people Using conjunctions	**Where I am a Local** In this video from National Geographic Learning, author Taiye Selasi talks about who she is, the places she comes from, and what it means to be a local somewhere.
Focused Listening: An Astronaut's Daily Life	Talking about Daily Schedules and Free Time Showing Interest Verbs that end in *-s*	When Your Hobby is also Your Job	Writing an Email to Make Plans Parts of an Email	**Ruben's Elevator** This film, from the National Geographic Short Film Showcase, gives a glimpse into the life of Ruben Pardo, the oldest manual elevator operator in Los Angeles, California.
General Listening: Conversations During Stages of Travel	Identifying Possession of Items Giving Personal Information for Travel Forms Asking for and Giving Advice Rising and Falling Intonation	Make Your Vacation More Interesting	Writing a Description of a Place Conjunctions: *because, so*	**The UK in 100 Seconds** In this film, National Geographic Explorer Daniel Raven-Ellison gives a look at the landscapes that make up the UK, and offers suggestions for how the use of land can be improved.
General and Focused Listening: Ordering a Meal in a Restaurant	Role-play: Ordering a Meal Talking about Quantities Reduced Forms: *Do you have...* and *Would you like...*	Urban Farming	Giving Instructions Sequencing Information	**A Guerilla Gardener in South Central LA** In this TED Talk, Ron Finley talks about LA Green Grounds, an organization he founded to show people in his neighborhood how to live a healthy and sustainable life that gives back to the community.
General and Focused Listening: Phone Calls about Everyday Activities and Today's Activities	Talking about What People are Doing Now Discussing Favorite Sports Talking about Likes and Dislikes Reduced Form: *What are you...*	eSports Go Global	Writing and Completing a Questionnaire Closed and Open Questions	**Free Soloing with Alex Honnold** In this video from National Geographic, climber and National Geographic Explorer Alex Honnold takes you up the massive Half Dome rock formation in Yosemite National Park in California... without a rope!
General Listening: Vacations and Weekend Trips	Describing and Comparing Vacations Asking about Your Weekend Discuss Where You Find Information Sounds of *-ed* Endings	The Cradle of the Inca Empire	Writing an Online Post Using Time References	**Vietnam's Green Jewels** This video from National Geographic gives information about the history and background of one of the world's most beautiful places: Vietnam's Ha Long Bay.

Listening	Speaking and Pronunciation	Reading	Writing	Video Journal
Focused Listening: A Voicemail, a Radio Call-In Show, and a Conversation	Asking for Contact Information Describing Sights, Sounds, and Other Sensations Giving Your Opinion Sentence Stress for Clarification	Do you Speak "Elephant"?	Writing Emails Asking for Information and Making Plans Formal and Informal Writing	**A New View of the Moon** In this video from National Geographic's Short Film Shortcase, filmmaker Wylie Overstreet takes a telescope to the city streets and asks people to look up and see the Moon in a new way.
General and Focused Listening: National Geographic Explorer Molly Ferrill Talks about her Latest Project	Talking about Short- and Long-Term Plans Make Predictions and Give Opinions about the Future Discussing a Personality Quiz Reduced form of *going to*	Electricity from the Sun	Analyzing Graphs to Describe Trends Writing to Describe Trends	**A Virtual Choir 2,000 Voices Strong** In this TED Talk, composer Eric Whitacre talks about the virtual choir, group of singers from around the world who come together online to make music and share their stories.
Focused Listening: A Conversation in a Shoe Store	Talking about Clothes Role-Play Different Shopping Experiences Stressed and Weak Syllables	Pride Through Fashion	Writing an Ad that Describes Clothes Describing Objects Adjective Order Punctuation	**How Your T-Shirt Can Make a Difference** In this video from National Geographic, the goods and resources that are used to make a T-shirt are shown, and a question is asked: How can your shopping and clothing care decisions make a difference?
General Listening: Personal Lifestyles and Habits	Discussing Healthy and Unhealthy Habits Asking and Telling about Lifestyles Approximation *Have to*	The Need for Sleep	Writing a Paragraph about a Healthy Hobby or Activity Paragraph Structure	**Living Past 100** In this video from National Geographic, the region of Bama, China, is profiled. It is one of the healthiest and most beautiful parts of the country.
Listening for General Understanding and Specific Details: Job Interviews	Interviewing for a Job Catching up with a Friend Using Present Perfect and Simple Past in Conversations Reduced Form of *have*	Being the First in Less Than Two Hours	Writing a Resume Checking for Mistakes in Writing	**Wasfia's Journey** In this video from National Geographic's Short Film Showcase, mountain climber, activist, and National Geographic Explorer Wasfia Nazreen talks about climbing the tallest mountain on each of the seven continents, and what her journey means to the people of her country.
Listening for Specific Details: A Podcast about a Trip that Didn't Waste Plastic Listening for Key Information	Discuss How to Save Money Talking about Choices Intonation	Crowdfunding for a Better World	Write an Email about a Major Decision Compare and Contrast	**Money Can't Buy You Happiness** In this video from National Geographic Learning, social scientist Michael Norton talks about the ways that money can, and can't, affect the well-being of us and the people around us.

Credits

vi (tl1) © Jelena Jankovic; (tl2) © Corey Arnold; (cl1) © Lorraine Yip; (cl2) © "The Hidden Garden" as seen in :The Art and Science of Cooking and the Modernist Cuisine Gallery, courtesy of The Cooking Lab, LLC.; (bl1) © Raul Jichici; (bl2) © Weng Sang Wong; **vii** (tl1) Dan Mullan/ Getty Images Sport/Getty Images; (tl2) © Mateo Boffano; (cl1) Tony Gentie/Reuters; (cl2) © Grant Thomas; (bl1) © Karla Gachet/Runa Photos; (bl2) © Carl David Granback; **001**(tl) Evgenia Pashkova/iStock/ Thinkstock; (tc) Gordine N/Shutterstock.com; (tc) Daxiao Productions/ Shutterstock.com; (tr) michaeljung/Shutterstock.com; (c) Digital Vision/ Alamy Stock Photo; (c) ColorBlind Images/Blend Images/Thinkstock; (c) Goodluz/Shutterstock.com; keellla/Shutterstock.com; **002** Minerva Studio/ Shutterstock.com; (bl) Gang Liu/Shutterstock.com; ESB Professional/ Shutterstock.com; (br) goodluz/Shutterstock.com; **004** Eric Rojas/ The New York Times/Redux; **006** STEVE DE NEEF/National Geographic Image Collection; **011** (tr) T photography/Shutterstock.com; (tr) solarseven/Shutterstock.com; (cr) wavebreakmedia/Shutterstock.com; (cr) Corbis Premium RF/Alamy Stock Photo; (cr) Timmary/Shutterstock. com; (cr) Evocation Images/Shutterstock.com; (br) Photographee. eu/Shutterstock.com; **012** Oleksandr Molotkovych/Shutterstock.com; (br) Roland Nagy/Alamy Stock Photo; (br) Rachel Moon/Shutterstock. com; **017** (tl) Ton Anurak/Shutterstock.com; (tc) Infinity21/Shutterstock. com; (tc) DreamPictures/Tetra images/Getty Images; (tl) Audtakorn Sutarmjam/EyeEm/Getty Images; (tc) PeopleImages/E+/Getty Images; (tc) mimagephotography/Shutterstock.com; (tr) JosuOzkaritz/iStock/Getty Images; (tr) Rattankun Thongbun/iStock/Getty Images; **020** Rob Wilson/ Shutterstock.com; **025** (tl) Artville/Getty Images; (tc) MayerKleinostheim/ iStock/Getty Images; (tc) Petr Malyshev/Shutterstock.com; (tr) Volosina/Shutterstock.com; (tl) Roman Samokhin/Shutterstock. com; (tc) PhotoDisc/Getty Images; (tc) MaraZe/Shutterstock.com; (tr) pikselstock/Shutterstock.com; **028** (tr) Digital Storm/Shutterstock.com; Olga Klochanko/Shutterstock.com; **030** © Cengage; **033** (tl) yanik88/ Shutterstock.com; (tc) Robert Kneschke/Shutterstock.com; (tr) Alexander Ishchenko/Shutterstock.com; (cl) takayuki/Shutterstock.com; Photodisc/ Getty Images; (cr) Greg Epperson/Shutterstock.com; **034** FatCamera/ E+/Getty Images; **035** (cl) Denis Pepin/Shutterstock.com; Andresr/ Shutterstock.com; (tc) iStock.com/ftwitty; (tr) Mike Flippo/Shutterstock. com; (tl) Prod-akszyn/Shutterstock.com; emmgunn/iStock/Getty Images; (tc) iStock.com/nicolas hansen; (cr) iStock.com/hero30; **036** tunart/E+/ Getty Images; **040** JIMMY CHIN/National Geographic Image Collection; **044** (b) Pixtal Images/Photolibrary (tr) Peter Hermes Furian/Shutterstock. com; **048** pavalena/Shutterstock.com; **049** (bl) Samuel Borges Photography/Shutterstock.com; (bc) chaoss/Shutterstock.com; (br) Valentin Valkov/Shutterstock.com; (bl) Bloomua/Shutterstock.com; (bc) Medioimages/Photodisc/Thinkstock; (br) BigLike Images/Shutterstock. com; **051** (tl) Colorburst/Dreamstime.com; (tc) Darren Baker/Shutterstock. com; (tc) Hurst Photo/Shutterstock.com; (tc) iStock.com/themacx; (tr) iStock.com/Maximastudio; **052** (tr) iStock.com/irvingnsaperstein; (cr) iStock.com/Alexandr Pakhnyushchyy; (bl) Ewan Chesser/Shutterstock. com; (br) iStock.com/Spydr; **053** Mr. Meijer/Shutterstock.com; **060** Beawiharta Beawiharta/Reutres; **066** iStock.com/jstudio; **067** (tl) Igor Grochev/Shutterstock.com; (tc) sumire8/Shutterstock.com; (tr) Alexander Kalina/Shutterstock.com; (tl) haveseen/Shutterstock.com; (tc) sagir/ Shutterstock.com; (tr) Tatiana Popova/Shutterstock.com; **068** Dinga/ Shutterstock.com; **070** Alexander Kalina/Shutterstock.com; **076** Racorn/ Shutterstock.com; **078** Galyna Andrushko/Shutterstock.com; **084** Karwai Tang/Getty Images Entertainment/Getty Images; **090** PrajitBoonpa/ Shutterstock.com; **092** (cl) Roy Hsu/Photographer's Choice/Getty Images; (br) Vilainecrevette/Shutterstock.com; (tl) Piotr Sikora/Shutterstock.com

People

UNIT 1

Lesson A Vocabulary and Grammar

A Look at the pictures. Complete the sentences with the words in the box.

chef	dancer	journalist	musician	photographer	pilot	police officer	students

1. He's a ________________.
2. She's a ________________.
3. He's a ________________.
4. She's a ________________.
5. She's a ________________.
6. He's a ________________.
7. They're ________________.
8. She's a ________________.

B Unscramble the country names to complete the sentences.

1. (nerladI) They're from ____________.
2. (eurP) I'm from ____________.
3. (aonrJd) She's from ____________.
4. (zalriB) He's from ____________.
5. (tSuho rAicaf) We're from ____________.
6. (rtasulAia) She's from ____________.
7. (coxMei) He's from ____________.
8. (aanpJ) They're from ____________.

C Match the questions and answers.

_______ **1.** Is he a musician?
_______ **2.** Are you a travel agent?
_______ **3.** Is Ellen from South Africa?
_______ **4.** Are Hana and Reo journalists?
_______ **5.** Is she a teacher?
_______ **6.** Are they from Ireland?

a. Yes, I am.
b. No, they're not. They're from Australia.
c. No, he's not.
d. Yes, they are.
e. Yes, she is.
f. No, she's a student.

A 2 Listen to the conversation. Complete the sentences.

Cristina: Where are you from, Mike?

Mike: I'm from (1) ________.

Cristina: So, you're (2) ________. Are you from Sydney?

Mike: Yes, I am. And you, Cristina? Are you (3) ________?

Cristina: No, I'm not. I'm (4) ________.

Mike: Wow! (5) ________! I'd love to go to your country. Which city are you from?

Cristina: I'm from Rio de Janeiro. It's a cool city!

B Circle the correct words to complete the sentences.

1. Lisa is from *England / English*. She's *England / English*.
2. Akita and Hiro are *Japan / Japanese*. They're from *Japan / Japanese*.
3. My friend Ramon is from *Mexico / Mexican*. He's *Mexico / Mexican*.
4. Rodrigo is *Chile / Chilean*. He's from *Chile / Chilean*.
5. I'm from *Peru / Peruvian*. I'm *Peru / Peruvian*.
6. They're from Toronto, *Canada / Canadian*. They're *Canada / Canadian*.
7. My friend is from *China / Chinese*. He's *China / Chinese*.
8. The teachers are *Ireland / Irish*. They're from *Ireland / Irish*.

C 3 Listen to four conversations. Complete the profiles.

1. **Name:** Maria Gutierrez
   Nationality: ________
   Country: ________
   Occupation: ________

2. **Name:** Dr. Matsuda
   Nationality: ________
   Country: ________
   Occupation: ________

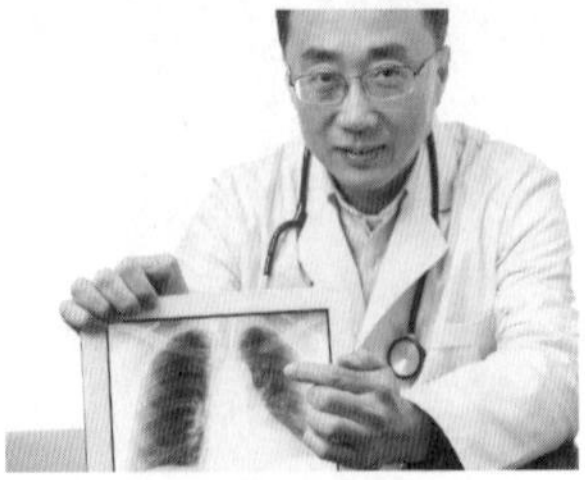

3. **Name:** Martina Flores
   Nationality: ________
   Country: ________
   Occupation: ________

4. **Name:** Luke Armstrong
   Nationality: ________
   Country: ________
   Occupation: ________

Lesson C Vocabulary and Grammar

A Circle the correct word to complete the questions.

1. *What* / *Where* are you from?
2. *What* / *Who* is her name?
3. *What* / *Where* do you do?
4. *What* / *How old* is your friend?
5. *Who* / *Where* is he from?
6. *What* / *Who* is your teacher?
7. *What* / *Where* is your nationality?
8. *What* / *Where* are the musicians?

B Match the opposites.

______	**1.** good	**a.** easy
______	**2.** rich	**b.** bad
______	**3.** boring	**c.** safe
______	**4.** happy	**d.** poor
______	**5.** dangerous	**e.** unhappy
______	**6.** difficult	**f.** interesting

C Complete the sentences with the correct form of *be*.

1. Jerry ______ a photographer. His job ______ interesting.
2. Dr. Valdez and Dr. Munoz ______ scientists.
3. Viktor's job ______ boring. He ______ sad.
4. You're a pilot? What ______ that like?
5. I ______ a teacher. My job ______ difficult.
6. She ______ a travel agent. Her job ______ boring sometimes.

D Circle the correct words to complete the sentences.

1. My job is *interesting* / *poor* / *happy*.
2. My classmates are *easy* / *happy* / *difficult*.
3. I'm a police officer. It's a(n) *dangerous* / *rich* / *sad* job.
4. Her job pays a very good salary. She's *boring* / *dangerous* / *rich*.
5. His job is easy, but sometimes it's *boring* / *rich* / *poor*.

E Unscramble the words to make sentences.

1. boring / Jean / person / is / a ______________________________
2. a / is / country / rich / Singapore ______________________________
3. baby / happy / my / a / is / daughter ______________________________
4. books / he / interesting / reads ______________________________
5. a / dangerous / the / place / is / city ______________________________
6. not / language / English / a / difficult / is ______________________________

No Boring Jobs

A good job is not always easy. Many people are happy with a job that is difficult but interesting. Read about three people like this.

Lara Setrakian is a journalist. She is from the United States, but travels to different parts of the world for her job. Sometimes, she is in places that are dangerous. Her job is difficult because she travels a lot. Her job is interesting because she meets many people from around the world. She talks with them about their lives, sometimes in their own language. She speaks five languages! They are English, Arabic, Armenian, French, and Spanish.

Misty Copeland is a dancer from the United States. She is a principal dancer with the American Ballet Theatre, in New York City. Principal dancers are the best dancers—male or female—in the company. Principal dancers earn a good salary. It is a difficult job. Misty practices for long hours and performs in many shows. She also travels to perform in other cities in the US and other countries.

José Andres is a chef. He is from Spain, but lives in the United States. He cooks Spanish food in good restaurants. He is also a **volunteer**. His **organization** is World Central Kitchen. He works with other chefs to give food to people in need all around the world. Sometimes, they help when there is a natural disaster, like in Puerto Rico and Haiti. In other countries, like Nicaragua and Cambodia, World Central Kitchen trains people to be chefs.

volunteer someone who chooses to do work he or she is not paid for

organization a group or association

Chef Jose Andres cooking for victims of Hurricane Maria in Puerto Rico

A Read the article. Circle **T** for *true* or **F** for *false*.

1. A good job is an easy job. T F
2. People with difficult jobs are always unhappy. T F
3. Lara, Misty, and Jose are all from the US. T F
4. Lara Setrakian is a photographer. T F
5. Misty Copeland is a good dancer. T F
6. A volunteer works without a salary. T F

B Answer the questions.

1. What is Lara Setrakian's job? ____________________
2. Is Lara's job safe or dangerous? ____________________
3. Where does Misty Copeland work? ____________________
4. Does her job pay a good salary? ____________________
5. What nationality is José Andres? ____________________
6. Where does he work? ____________________

C Check (✓) the correct columns, according to the reading.

This person...	**Lara Setrakian**	**Misty Copeland**	**José Andres**
is from the United States.			
travels for work.			
is a volunteer.			
earns a good salary.			

D Write two adjectives to describe each job.

1. journalist ____________________
2. dancer ____________________
3. chef ____________________

A Read the personal description. Answer the questions.

The man in the photo is Brian Skerry. He is from the United States. He is a photographer. He is a National Geographic Explorer. He takes pictures of sperm whales. He is not a scientist. He takes photos to help scientists research and learn about sperm whales. He travels all over the world to take pictures of the whales.

1. What is his name? ____________________
2. Where is he from? ____________________
3. What is his job? ____________________

B Look at the photo and read the paragraph in **A** again. Write sentences about Brian Skerry's job using these adjectives.

1. easy ____________________
2. difficult ____________________
3. dangerous ____________________
4. boring ____________________
5. interesting ____________________
6. safe ____________________

C Circle the correct words to complete the sentences. In one sentence, both options are correct.

1. Brian Skerry is a photographer, *and* / *but* not a scientist.
2. He is a photographer *and* / *but* a National Geographic Explorer.
3. He is from the United States *and* / *but* he travels all over the world.
4. He takes photos *and* / *but* helps scientists.
5. Scientists research *and* / *but* learn about sperm whales.

Conjunctions

And is for extra information.

But is for different information.

D Complete the description of Brian Skerry with the words in the box.

and	but	dangerous	interesting

The man in the photo is Brian Skerry. He is from the United States. He is a photographer (1) ____________ a National Geographic Explorer. He takes pictures of sperm whales. His job is (2) ____________ but (3) ____________. He works with scientists, (4) ____________ he isn't a scientist. He takes photos to help scientists research and learn about sperm whales.

Review

A Complete the sentences with the correct form of *be*. Use contractions where possible.

1. Hello! I _______ Yong-Min.
2. Ms. Costa _______ a photographer. Her job _______ very interesting.
3. They _______ journalists. They _______ from Brazil and Chile.
4. You _______ a dancer! What's that like?
5. He _______ a teacher. His name _______ Mr. Clark.
6. Mr. Shen _______ from China. He _______ an engineer.

B Write the second sentence in each item using a contraction and the nationality.

1. He is from Ireland. He's Irish______________________.
2. They are from Japan. ______________________________.
3. We are from Chile. ______________________________.
4. I am from England. ______________________________.
5. She is from Peru. ______________________________.
6. You are from Australia. ______________________________.

C Unscramble the words to make questions.

1. your / what / name / is ______________________________?
2. from / you / are / where ______________________________?
3. you / what / do / do ______________________________?
4. work / is / your / interesting ______________________________?
5. friends / are / your / who ______________________________?
6. she / how / is / old ______________________________?

D Complete the sentences.

1. Diem is *happy* / *unhappy*. She has a *good* / *rich* job.
2. Elena is sad. Her job is *boring* / *interesting*.
3. My father is a police officer. It's a *dangerous* / *poor* job.
4. She's a pilot. She has an interesting but *easy* / *difficult* job.
5. We're travel agents. Sometimes, our job is *interesting* / *unhappy*.

Video Where I am a local

A Complete the sentences so they are true for you.

1. The question "Where are you from?" is *easy / difficult* to answer.

2. The question "Where do you feel at home?" is *easy / difficult* to answer.

B Watch the video. Number the sentences in the order you hear them.

_______ **a.** Currently, I am living in Paris.

_______ **b.** I am from Porto, which is in the north of Portugal.

_______ **c.** I'm from Paris.

_______ **d.** I am from Barcelona.

_______ **e.** I am from Mexico City.

C Watch the video. Check the questions you hear.

_______ **1.** Where are you from?

_______ **2.** What country are you from?

_______ **3.** Where is your home?

_______ **4.** Where do you feel at home?

_______ **5.** Am I from Ghana?

_______ **6.** Am I from the United Kingdom?

_______ **7.** Am I from Nigeria?

_______ **8.** Am I from the US?

_______ **9.** Am I from Portugal?

_______ **10.** Where are you a local?

D In the video, a person says, "I identify myself as from Portugal, not from a single city." Do you identify yourself as from your whole country, or from one part of it? Why?

____

____

____

____

____

____

____

____

A Day in the Life

UNIT 2

Lesson A Vocabulary and Grammar

A Match the columns to create collocations.

_______ **1.** brush **a.** work
_______ **2.** eat **b.** the bus
_______ **3.** catch **c.** coffee
___g___ **4.** go to **d.** break
_______ **5.** take a **e.** your teeth
_______ **6.** start **f.** lunch
_______ **7.** drink **g.** the movies

B Number the activities in order (1–4).

_______ **a.** Next, she has lunch with her coworkers.
_______ **b.** Finally, she leaves work at the end of the day.
_______ **c.** Then she starts work at 8:30 a.m.
_______ **d.** First, Monica catches the bus.

C Put the words in order to make sentences.

1. at / eat / you / o'clock / do / one / lunch ____________________________________?
2. bed / he / time / go / what / does / to ____________________________________?
3. o'clock / up / she / at / gets / seven ____________________________________.
4. break / don't / I / in the afternoon / a / take ____________________________________.
5. she / in the morning / coffee / does / drink ____________________________________?
6. children / school / at / do / your / three / leave / o'clock ____________________________________?
7. showers / they / do / in the evening / take ____________________________________?
8. at / don't / class / go to / ten thirty / I ____________________________________.

D Complete the conversations with *do*, *does*, *doesn't*, or *don't*. Use capital letters as needed.

1. A: __________ Erica start work at eight o'clock?
B: No, she __________. She starts work at eight thirty.
2. A: __________ you and your family have dinner at six thirty?
B: Yes, we __________.
3. A: __________ you drink tea or coffee in the morning?
B: I drink tea. I __________ drink coffee.
4. A: What time __________ Miguel go to class?
B: He goes to class at nine thirty.
5. A: __________ the students always finish their homework?
B: No, they __________.
6. A: __________ she eat breakfast in the morning?
B: No, she __________.
7. A: __________ they finish class at four o'clock?
B: No, they __________. They finish at four fifteen.

Lesson B Listening

A 5 Listen and answer the questions.

1. What does Pedro ask Sasha about?
   a. How to get exercise **b.** Their homework **c.** Her free time
2. When does Sasha do the activities she talks about?
   a. Saturday afternoon **b.** Sunday morning **c.** Saturday morning
3. What does Sasha do after she drinks coffee?
   a. She takes a shower. **b.** She meets friends. **c.** She goes walking.
4. Who does more activities in their free time?
   a. Pedro **b.** Sasha
5. Does Sasha get exercise on the weekend?
   a. Yes, she does. **b.** No, she doesn't.
6. What does Sasha say about the gym?
   a. It's difficult. **b.** It's boring. **c.** It's safe.
7. What does Sasha tell Pedro to do?
   a. Go running in the park **b.** Do his homework **c.** Come walking with her

B Complete the sentences with the correct form of *go* or *go to*.

1. I ______ running in the park in the afternoon.
2. Do the students always ______ the library after class?
3. Do you ______ shopping on the weekends?
4. They ______ the movies on Friday night.
5. We don't ______ swimming at night.
6. Dan ______ work at eight o'clock.
7. They ______ the Chinese restaurant sometimes.
8. She ______ dancing on the weekends.

C 6 Circle the correct words. Then listen and check your answers.

1. Edgar goes shopping on Saturday morning, *and / but* so does Linda.
2. My son plays piano, and *neither / so* does my daughter.
3. I don't do homework on the weekend, and *neither / so* do you.
4. Elena eats out on Saturday night, *and / but* Nicole doesn't.
5. Marie doesn't exercise on Sunday morning, and *neither / so* does Carlos.
6. Oscar watches TV on Sunday evening, and *neither / so* does his son.

Lesson C Vocabulary and Grammar

A Look at the pictures. Complete the sentences.

celebrate	costumes	decorate	festivals
fireworks	party	presents	

1. People dress up in __________ for Carnival in Brazil.
2. There are always __________ on New Year's Eve.
3. In the US, people __________ Independence Day.
4. The children are at a birthday __________.
5. People often receive __________ on their birthday.
6. Street __________ are popular in the summer.
7. People __________ the house for a party.

1

2

3

4

5

6

7

B Circle the correct word to complete the sentence.

1. My graduation *party* / *festival* is on Sunday.
2. How do you *celebrate* / *decorate* the New Year?
3. The *costumes* / *fireworks* are always at night.
4. My parents give me *presents* / *costumes* on my birthday.
5. The Primavera Sound music *costume* / *festival* happens in Barcelona every year.
6. She *decorated* / *celebrated* the table with flowers.
7. The dancers wear masks and *costumes* / *presents* on stage.

C Write the correct adverb of frequency on each line.

__________ __________ __________ __________ __________

0 percent ←——————————————→ 100 percent

always	never	often
sometimes	usually	

D Write the sentences again using the adverbs of frequency.

1. I visit my family on Thanksgiving. (usually)

   ____

2. American Independence Day is on July 4. (always)

   ____

3. We work on New Year's Day. (never)

   ____

4. It is cold in winter. (usually)

   ____

5. We give presents to our friends. (often)

   ____

Happy New Year!

In the Netherlands, New Year's Day is always on January 1. It's very cold, so **Dutch** people stay home and clean their houses. They have a party and eat sweet bread and donuts. In the evening, they watch a funny TV show and then there are fireworks.

The Chinese New Year celebration is in January or February. The date is different every year. It's a big festival that lasts for 15 days. People don't go to work. They clean their houses and decorate doors for good luck. People give presents and money in red envelopes. They eat big dinners with their families. At night, they watch fireworks.

In Iran, New Year's Day is called Nowruz, and it's in March. The festival begins on the first day of spring and continues for almost two weeks. Nowruz is one of the most important holidays in Iran. Before the holiday, people clean their houses and buy new clothes. People put seven special things, including apples, coins, garlic, and grass, on their tables. Iranians visit everyone in their families and eat special meals. Adults give presents, such as money or gold, to children.

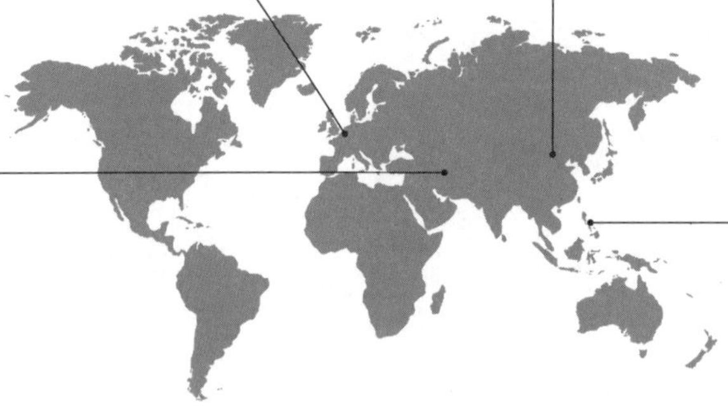

In the Philippines, the New Year starts on January 1. People begin to celebrate the night before. They decorate the table with **round** foods such as apples and grapes. People also wear clothes with polka dots. They think that round things, like fruit, polka dots, and coins, bring good luck for the new year. It is a fun and noisy holiday with fireworks at midnight.

Dutch from the Netherlands
round circle shaped

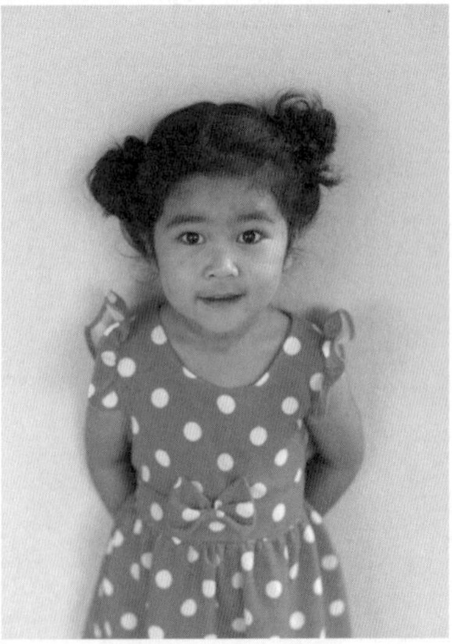

▲ A young girl wears a polka dot dress.

▲ Fireworks in Manila, Philippines, on New Year's Eve

A Which country is it? Check (✓) the answers. You can have one, two, or three answers for each sentence.

New Year Celebrations	The Netherlands	Iran	China	The Philippines
1. People eat special food.				
2. People watch fireworks.				
3. It's always in January.				
4. People give presents.				
5. It's a long celebration.				
6. People watch TV.				
7. People clean their houses.				

B Circle **T** for *true* or **F** for *false*.

1. In the Netherlands, people give presents. T F
2. In the Netherlands, they don't have a big dinner. T F
3. People put apples on the table in Iran and the Philippines. T F
4. In Iran, children give gifts to adults. T F
5. In China, the red envelopes don't have money inside. T F
6. People decorate their doors in China. T F
7. In China, people decorate tables with round things. T F
8. In the Philippines, there are flowers on the table. T F

C Circle the incorrect options.

1. People watch TV. *Iran / Netherlands / Philippines*
2. New Year's is always the same day. *China / Iran / Philippines*
3. Round things are for good luck. *China / Netherlands / Philippines*
4. People put special things on the table. *China / Iran / Philippines*
5. People watch fireworks. *China / Iran / Netherlands*
6. People visit their families. *China / Iran / Netherlands*
7. The celebration lasts more than two days. *China / Iran / Philippines*
8. People give money. *China / Iran / Netherlands*

D Complete the sentences. Use your own ideas.

1. On New Year's Day, I ______________________________
____
______________________________.

2. I would like to celebrate New Year's Day in (the Netherlands / Iran / China / the Philippines) because ______
____
______________________________.

Lesson E Writing

A Match the parts of the email with the words and phrases.

_______ **1.** Start the email
_______ **2.** Ask for help
_______ **3.** Ask for information
_______ **4.** Arrange to meet
_______ **5.** End the email

a. Let's meet at 1:30.
b. See you later.
c. Can you bring...
d Hi Miguel,
e. Do you know what time...

B Complete the email with the words and phrases in **A**.

____

We have the day off from school on Thursday because it's Thanksgiving. Do you want to eat with my family and me that day? We have a big meal.

On Thanksgiving Day, I get up early and help my mother and grandmother make a special dinner. The whole family comes to our house. Sometimes, there are more than 20 people! People usually bring a vegetable dish or dessert, like a pie. ____________________ some food from your country?

We eat at about 2 o'clock. ____________________ the buses run on holidays?
____________________ at my house. You can meet everyone before we eat.

____

Ken

C Write an email to a friend or classmate. Invite him or her to a celebration in your country. Include the five parts of an email from **A**.

____

____

____

____

____

____

____

Review

A Use the words to write questions with *do* or *does* and a verb to write questions about daily activities.

1. what time / she / breakfast What time does she eat breakfast?
2. what time / you / a shower ____________________?
3. what time / they / lunch ____________________?
4. what time / they / school ____________________?
5. he / to class / in the afternoon ____________________?
6. they / the bus / at 7:20 ____________________?
7. your classmates / a break / at 10:00 ____________________?
8. you / your teeth / at night ____________________?

B Complete the questions and answers with *do*, *does*, *don't*, or *doesn't*.

1. **A:** ________ the students and teachers take a break at 10:30?
   B: Yes, they ________.
2. **A:** What time ________ she go to a meeting?
   B: At 10:30 a.m.
3. **A:** ________ the teacher drink coffee in class?
   B: No, she ________.
4. **A:** ________ you eat lunch at school?
   B: No, I ________. I eat lunch at home.
5. **A:** ________ your sister always get up at 7:30?
   B: Yes, she ________.
6. **A:** ________ the students eat lunch in the classroom?
   B: No, they ________.

C Complete the sentences with *so*, *but*, or *neither*.

1. Filipino people celebrate the new year in January, ________ Iranian people don't.
2. Dutch people clean their houses for the new year, and ________ do the Chinese.
3. Filipinos don't decorate their doors, and ________ do Iranians.
4. The new year festival in Iran lasts almost two weeks, ________ in the Netherlands it doesn't.
5. The Netherlands celebrates New Year's Day on January 1, and ________ does the Philippines.
6. The Philippines, the Netherlands, and China celebrate the new year with fireworks, ________ Iran doesn't.
7. People in the Netherlands don't give presents, and ________ do people in the Philippines.
8. Iranians decorate the table with special things, and ________ do Filipinos.

Video Ruben's Elevator

A Answer the questions.

1. Do you usually say "hello" to people in an elevator? ____________________
2. When you're in an elevator, where do you look? At the floor? At the door? At the other people?

   ____
3. Have you ever been in an elevator with an elevator operator? If yes, where? ____________________

B Complete the paragraph.

1976	age nine	classic movies	elevator operator	free time
friendly	laughs	powerful	story	

Ruben Pardo is an (1) ____________________. He started his job in (2) ____________________. He is a (3) ____________________ man who talks with the people who ride the elevator. He (4) ____________________ a lot. Ruben's life wasn't easy. He started working at (5) ____________________ to help his family. But Ruben thinks about positive things. People are very important to him. He says, "We're so many people. And yet, none of us have the same situation. Isn't that very (6) ____________________? I mean, everybody has a (7) ____________________." In his (8) ____________________, Ruben enjoys (9) ____________________ and going to restaurants with his family.

C Write the verb from the box that means the same as the underlined word(s).

guarantees	notice	observed	recommends	sacrificed	situation

1. As a child, Ruben <u>watched</u> the elevator operators doing their jobs. ____________________
2. Ruben wants the viewer to <u>see</u> that the elevator and second floor are level. ____________________
3. Ruben <u>gave up</u> his education to help his brother and sisters. ____________________
4. Ruben talks about his <u>job and the things that are happening now.</u> ____________________
5. He <u>says it's important</u> that everyone should look forward to something. ____________________
6. Ruben <u>promises</u> that he will run the elevator in the future. ____________________

D Answer the questions.

1. Ruben Pardo describes his job as "serving the public." He sees many people for a couple of minutes each day. What other jobs can you think of like this?

   ____________________.
2. Think of your answer in question 1. Does learning about Ruben change your ideas about talking with people you only see for a short time each day, like a bus driver?

   ____________________.

   ____________________.

Going Places

UNIT 3

Lesson A Vocabulary and Grammar

A Look at the pictures. Complete the sentences.

carry-on bag	charger	check-in desk	exchange	packing luggage	passport	sunblock	take a taxi

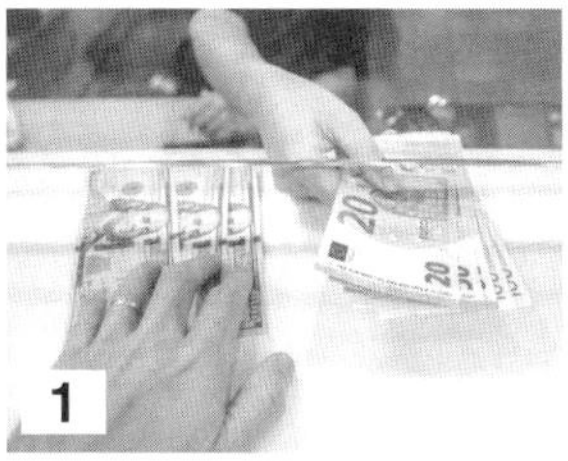

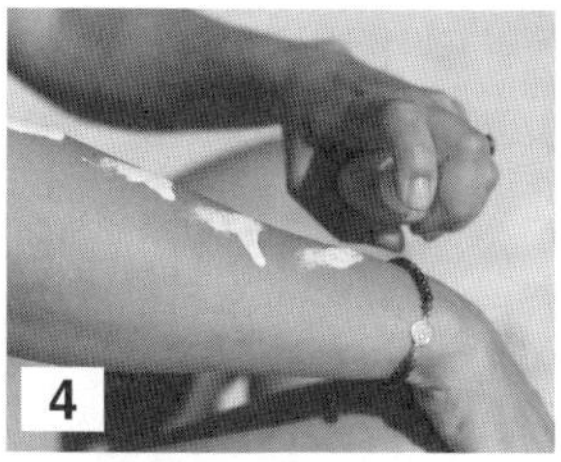

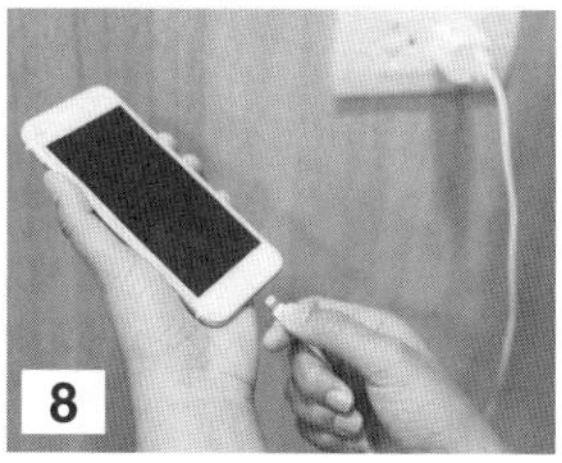

1. ________________ money at the airport.
2. Show your ________________ at the check-in desk.
3. It's expensive to ________________ to the airport.
4. You need ________________ for the beach.
5. She is ________________ for a trip.
6. At the airport, first go to the ________________.
7. He has a ________________ and a suitcase.
8. My phone ________________ is in my carry-on bag.

B Put the activities in order (1–8).

Before you fly

_____ **a.** Go to the check-in desk.
_____ **b.** Check your luggage.
_____ **c.** Pack your luggage.
_____ **d.** Get to the airport on time.

After you arrive

_____ **e.** Wait for your luggage.
_____ **f.** Exchange your money.
_____ **g.** Show your passport.
_____ **h.** Take a taxi to your hotel.

C Match the sentences.

_____ **1.** It's your bag.
_____ **2.** It's my passport.
_____ **3.** They're our tickets.
_____ **4.** It's their luggage.
_____ **5.** It's his suitcase.

a. They belong to us.
b. It belongs to them.
c. It belongs to him.
d. It belongs to me.
e. It belongs to you.

Lesson B Listening

A 8 Listen and answer the questions.

1. Where is the man traveling to?
   a. Miami b. Atlanta c. Columbus
2. What identification does the man give the woman?
   a. his passport b. his driver's license c. his credit card
3. How many bags does the man have?
   a. one suitcase b. two suitcases and a carry-on c. one suitcase and a carry-on
4. What does the woman ask the man?
   a. Do you have anything that belongs to someone else?
   b. Are you traveling with someone else?
   c. Do you have a laptop in your bag?
5. Whose things are in the suitcase?
   a. his and his wife's b. his c. a friend's
6. Why does the man put his carry-on bag into a box?
   a. to make sure it's not too small
   b. to make sure it's not too heavy
   c. to make sure it's not too big

B Unscramble the words to make questions.

1. you / a single / would / or / like / a double room ____________________?
2. leave / do / the 14th / on / or / you / the 15th ____________________?
3. that / do / a K / a C / spell / with / you / or ____________________?
4. you / to pay / or / by cash / want / do / by card ____________________?
5. my / do / passport / you / need ____________________?
6. pleasure / are / for business / traveling / or / you ____________________?

C 9 Listen. Write the information you hear.

1. First name ____________________
2. Middle initial(s) ____________________
3. Last name ____________________
4. Date of birth ____________________
5. Nationality ____________________
6. Country of residence ____________________
7. Contact number ____________________
8. Number of nights ____________________

Lesson C Vocabulary and Grammar

A Match the opposites.

______	**1.** cold	**a.** expensive
______	**2.** crowded	**b.** ugly
______	**3.** cheap	**c.** safe
______	**4.** beautiful	**d.** quiet
______	**5.** dangerous	**e.** hot

B Read the first sentence. Then circle *should* or *shouldn't* in the second.

1. That neighborhood is dangerous. Tourists *should* / *shouldn't* walk there late at night.
2. New York City is cold in the winter. He *should* / *shouldn't* pack warm clothes.
3. *Alfajores* are delicious Argentinian cookies. You *should* / *shouldn't* try one!
4. The new hotel is very expensive. We *should* / *shouldn't* stay there.
5. The market is very crowded on Saturday. You *should* / *shouldn't* go on a weekday.
6. Santiago is very beautiful. She *should* / *shouldn't* take a lot of photos.
7. The weather is sunny in Florida. We *should* / *shouldn't* pack our sunglasses.
8. The trains between cities are fast. They *should* / *shouldn't* rent a car.

C Ask for advice. Read the responses and write questions.

1. Q: ______________________________? **A:** Yes, you should. The food at Calisto's Cafe is delicious.
2. Q: ______________________________? **A:** No, you shouldn't. Gifts at the airport are expensive.
3. Q: ______________________________? **A:** Yes, you should. It is cold at night.
4. Q: ______________________________? **A:** No, you shouldn't visit Boston City Hall. It's ugly.
5. Q: ______________________________? **A:** Yes, you should go with a friend. It's dangerous alone.
6. Q: ______________________________? **A:** Yes, you should take a camera. The beach is beautiful.

D Unscramble the words to make questions.

1. pack / need / to / warm / I / clothes / do ______________________________?
2. to Kyoto / we / don't / why / train / the / take ______________________________?
3. a reservation / is / to make / a / good idea / it ______________________________?
4. to visit / need / a visa / Brazil / I / do ______________________________?
5. my cell phone / should / I / bring ______________________________?
6. to go / safe / it / at night / is / there ______________________________?
7. me / you / some advice / could / give ______________________________?
8. hotel / cheap / we / in / should / stay / a ______________________________?

Travel Light!

Even on a long trip, you don't need a lot of heavy suitcases. You only need two bags—a carry-on bag and a check-in bag. Here is some advice for packing them.

Carry-on bag

- Your carry-on bag should be small and light.
- The most important things for your trip (passport, boarding pass, airline tickets, money, credit cards, cell phone, keys, etc.) should go in your carry-on bag.
- You should pack valuable things, such as a laptop or jewelry, in your carry-on bag.
- You should bring a change of clothes in case your luggage is delayed.
- You should also take any medicine you need in your carry-on bag.
- Bring snacks to eat on the plane. Cookies, nuts, and dried fruit are good. Don't bring chocolate—it's very messy. For long trips, bring a sandwich. And don't bring water—you can't take it through security. You should buy some at the airport before you board the plane.
- Remember to bring a good book or your tablet.

Check-in bag

- Your check-in bag should be strong.
- Your clothes, shoes, and other everyday things should go in your check-in bag.
- Make a list to help you remember everything.
- Pack your bag early—don't pack on the same day as your trip!
- Think about the weather. Do you need a coat and gloves, or T-shirts and shorts? Choose the right clothes! You should pack your clothes inside plastic bags.
- Put your name and your hotel's address and telephone number on your bag. You should put this information inside the bag, too.

A Circle **T** for *true* or **F** for *false*.

1. You need three bags to go on a trip.	T	F
2. Your carry-on bag should be big and strong.	T	F
3. Your carry-on bag is for things you need on the airplane.	T	F
4. Your check-in bag is for clothes and things you use on your vacation.	T	F
5. You should put your home address on your check-in bag.	T	F
6. You should pack your laptop in your check-in bag.	T	F
7. You shouldn't take food in your carry-on bag.	T	F
8. You should put your clothes in plastic bags.	T	F

B Are these things you should or shouldn't do?

	Should do	Shouldn't do
1. Pack your bags a few days before your trip.		
2. Put your keys in your carry-on bag.		
3. Get information about the weather before you pack.		
4. Pack chocolate in your carry-on bag.		
5. Bring water in your bags.		
6. Put your name on your bag.		
7. Bring a sandwich with you.		
8. Put your credit card in your check in bag.		

C Read the advice. Is it for the carry-on bag or the check-in bag? Write which bag.

1. You should pack any medicine you need in this bag. ____________
2. You should put magazines in this bag. ____________
3. You should pack your swimsuit in this bag. ____________
4. You should put headphones in this bag. ____________

D Write the things you pack in your bags for a trip.

Carry-on bag	Check-in bag

Lesson E Writing

A Complete the sentences with *because* or *so*.

1. Some travelers check in online __________ it saves time.
2. A lot of tourists visit Barcelona, __________ it is crowded.
3. Paris is a beautiful city, __________ millions of tourists visit each year.
4. Hotels are very expensive in July __________ the festival is during that month.
5. He's going to Buenos Aires __________ it's an interesting place for sightseeing.
6. You can't rent a car __________ you don't have a driver's license.
7. The flight to Santiago is nine hours, __________ you should pack food in your carry-on bag.
8. Some people go camping __________ they enjoy nature.

B Complete the sentences with your own ideas. Use *because* or *so* in each sentence.

1. There are many beautiful things to see, so you should bring your camera.
2. The street food in Rio de Janeiro is delicious, ____________________.
3. The bus is crowded in the morning ____________________.
4. The flight is six hours long, ____________________.
5. The tickets are expensive ____________________.
6. You should check the website ____________________.

C Circle the correct words to complete the paragraph.

The Alhambra in Granada, Spain, is a *beautiful* / *warm* castle. It's a popular place to visit, *because* / *so* it is usually *crowded* / *quiet*. Many tourists visit the Alhambra, *because* / *so* you should buy your tickets in advance online. It is important to buy tickets before you arrive *because* / *so* only a certain number of people can visit each day. You should go in the morning *because* / *so* the sun is very *hot* / *cold* in the afternoon. You should wear sunblock and a hat *because* / *so* some of the sights are outside. You should take a camera *because* / *so* the Alhambra is a great place for photos.

D Write a paragraph giving advice to someone who is visiting a place you know. Tell them things they *should* and *shouldn't* do there. Give reasons for the advice. Use the conjunctions *because* and *so*.

____

____

____

____

____

____

____

Review

A Unscramble the words to make statements and questions.

1. money / shouldn't / pack / in / you / your / check-in bag ______________________.
2. credit card / pay / should / your / with / you ______________________.
3. money / at a bank / we / should / exchange ______________________?
4. you / put / shouldn't / our / in / the check-in bag / medicine ______________________.
5. I / stay / hotel / a / cheap / should / at ______________________?
6. every day / eat at / you / restaurants / shouldn't / expensive ______________________.
7. go / you / in / the morning / should / shopping ______________________.
8. early / crowded / because / go / to the airport / you / should / it's ______________________.

B Complete the sentences with the correct possessive adjective and possessive pronoun. Use the words to write questions and answers.

1. camera / his Whose camera is it? It's his. It belongs to him.
2. sunglasses / mine ______________________
3. phone charger / ours ______________________
4. carry-on bag / yours ______________________
5. book / hers ______________________
6. luggage / theirs ______________________

C Circle the correct word to complete the sentences.

1. The hotel is in a *safe* / *warm* part of the city.
2. There are a lot of *expensive* / *delicious* stores on 5th Avenue, in New York.
3. The train is very *crowded* / *beautiful* on Friday evenings.
4. Tourists visit the Alhambra because it is *beautiful* / *ugly*.
5. Early in the morning, the beach is *crowded* / *quiet*.
6. Take a taxi because the subway is *dangerous* / *safe* at night.
7. Pack a coat, hat, and gloves because Toronto is *cold* / *hot* in winter.
8. Try the seafood because it's *delicious* / *ugly*.

D Complete the sentences with *should* or *shouldn't*.

1. They __________ go to the pizza restaurant. It's always crowded.
2. You __________ walk there alone at night. It's dangerous.
3. __________ we go early in the morning?
4. We __________ ask someone for advice. They can help us.
5. You __________ fly. You should take the train.
6. I __________ bring sunblock because it will be very hot.

Video The UK in 100 Seconds

A Before you watch, try to guess what the UK looks like. Number the parts from largest (1) to smallest (6) area.

_______ **a.** peat bogs
_______ **b.** fields with animals
_______ **c.** forest
_______ **d.** grasslands and moors
_______ **e.** cities and towns
_______ **f.** fields with crops

B Watch the video. Check your ideas in **A**. Then write the correct number next to each kind of land.

_______ % **1.** peat bogs
_______ % **2.** fields with animals
_______ % **3.** forest
_______ % **4.** grasslands and moors
_______ % **5.** cities and towns
_______ % **6.** fields with crops

C Match the word from the video with its meaning.

_______ **1.** moors
_______ **2.** peat bogs
_______ **3.** fuel
_______ **4.** crops
_______ **5.** cover

a. wet land with dead plant material
b. to be over or on top of something
c. large areas with grass and plants that is not good for farming
d. something you burn to produce energy
e. plants for food

D After you watch, think about the types of land uses in the UK. Did the percentage of land for cities and towns surprise you? Why?

____
____
____
____
____
____
____

Food

UNIT 4

Lesson A Vocabulary and Grammar

A Label the foods. Use the plural form as needed.

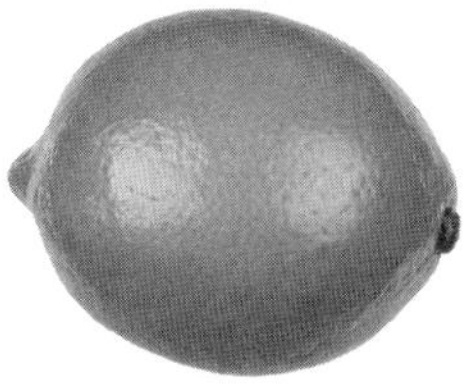

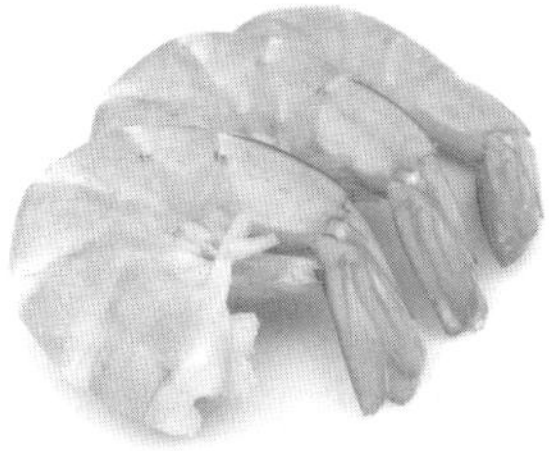

1. ________ **2.** ________ **3.** ________ **4.** ________

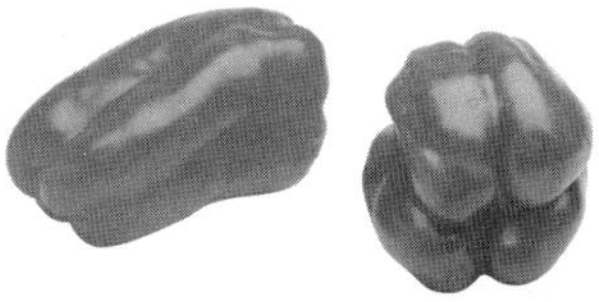

5. ________ **6.** ________ **7.** ________ **8.** ________

B Cross out the words that do not belong.

1. **dairy products** cheese, butter, coffee, milk
2. **drinks** oranges, water, soda, tea
3. **fruit** apples, bananas, eggs, lemons
4. **meat** steak, turkey bacon, potatoes, chicken
5. **vegetables** lettuce, peppers, onions, shrimp

C Write sentences with *This is*, *This is a/an*, or *These are*, and the food given.

1. (apple) This is an apple.
2. (chicken) ________
3. (egg) ________
4. (potatoes) ________
5. (sausages) ________
6. (orange) ________

D Circle the correct word to complete the sentence.

1. There aren't *any* / *some* tomatoes.
2. There are *any* / *some* onions.
3. This is *a* / *an* old apple.
4. There are *any* / *some* oranges.
5. There is *a* / *an* banana in the fruit bowl.
6. There is *any* / *some* sugar on the table.
7. She needs *any* / *some* olive oil for the recipe.
8. There isn't *any* / *some* shrimp at the store.

A 11 Listen to the conversation. Circle the correct answer.

1. Does the server say her name and the name of the restaurant?
   a. yes **b.** no
2. What is the first question the server asks?
   a. How are you tonight? **b.** Are you ready to order? **c.** Would you like something to drink?
3. What appetizer does the man order?
   a. garden salad **b.** Greek salad **c.** soup
4. What main dish does the woman order?
   a. shrimp **b.** chicken **c.** fish
5. What is one of the side dishes the woman orders?
   a. French fries **b.** salad **c.** potatoes
6. What is the last thing they order?
   a. shrimp **b.** French fries **c.** soup

B 12 Read the sentences. Does a server or customer usually say this? Write *S* or *C*. Then listen and check your answers.

1. Would you like French fries or a salad with that? ___
2. For the main dish, I would like cheese pizza. ___
3. Do you have green tea? ___
4. How would you like the steak? ___
5. Does the omelet come with a side salad? ___
6. Can I have a glass of water, please? ___
7. Is the sausage spicy? ___
8. What would you like to drink? ___

C A server and a customer are in a restaurant. Unscramble the sentences in their conversation.

1. are / order / ready / you / to
   Server: ____?
2. recommend / what / you / would
   Customer: ____?
3. excellent / the / chicken / is
   Server: ____.
4. come / does / chicken / with / salad / the
   Customer: ____?
5. does / yes / it
   Server: ____.
6. a baked potato / have / I'll / the / and / chicken
   Customer: ____.
7. like / would / else / you / anything
   Server: ____?
8. like / I / a / glass / of / would / mineral water
   Customer: ____.

Lesson C Vocabulary and Grammar

A Read the sentences. Circle the correct answer.

1. I eat a lot of ________. I like eggplant, carrots, and onions.
   a. vegetarian b. fresh c. vegetables
2. A ________ diet includes beans, brown rice, vegetables, and wheat bread.
   a. high-fiber b. high-protein c. home grown
3. She eats ________ vegetables from her garden all summer.
   a. frozen b. processed c. home grown
4. Kenji is a(n) ________. He doesn't eat meat, but he eats dairy products.
   a. vegan b. vegetarian c. organic
5. Eating a lot of ________ is not good for you.
   a. fresh b. home grown c. fast food
6. A ________ diet includes chicken, fish, and eggs.
   a. fast food b. high-protein c. vegan

B Circle the correct word.

1. **A:** How *much* / *many* cheese do you need?
   B: *A lot* / *A few*. I'm making six pizzas.
2. **A:** How *much* / *many* sausages do we have?
   B: Not *many* / *much*. There are two in the fridge.
3. **A:** How *much* / *many* milk do you usually buy?
   B: *A lot* / *a little* because I have four kids.
4. **A:** How *much* / *many* sugar do you put in your tea?
   B: Not *many* / *much*. Just a little.
5. **A:** How *much* / *many* burgers are there?
   B: Only *a lot* / *a few*. We need to buy more.
6. **A:** How *much* / *many* rice do you want?
   B: Not *many* / *much*. I'm on a high-protein diet.
7. **A:** How *much* / *many* desserts do we need?
   B: Not *many* / *much*. My friends are very healthy.
8. **A:** How *much* / *many* oranges do you need to make the juice?
   B: *A lot* / *A few*. Everyone wants some.

C Complete the sentences with *much*, *many*, *a lot*, *a little*, or *a few*.

1. People on high-protein diets eat ________ of meat and fish.
2. Ritika doesn't eat ________ wheat bread. She doesn't like the taste.
3. We have ________ of apples. Let's make a pie!
4. How ________ tomatoes do we need?
5. How ________ garlic do you put in the sauce?
6. Put ________ salt in the soup. Not too much!
7. Carla only eats ________ chocolate every day.
8. Can you eat nuts? The salad has ________ walnuts in it.

Making Good Food Choices

How much dairy should you eat every day? How many glasses of water do I need every day? How much protein do we need? There are so many popular diets that it's hard to know what is healthy. Some countries produce charts with information and pictures to help people make healthy food choices.

The chart from the United States looks like a plate and a glass. There are five food groups: fruits, **grains**, dairy, vegetables, and protein. The size of each food group shows how much you need each day. Vegetables and grains are the largest sections. These are the foods you should eat a lot of every day. Also, you need to eat some protein, such as meat, fish, or eggs, and some fruits. The dairy section is the smallest. That means you shouldn't eat a lot of dairy products, such as milk, yogurt, or cheese. The chart doesn't say how much sugar or fat you should eat, or how much water to drink.

The food balance chart in Korea is the shape of a bicycle! It has six food groups and water. In addition to the food groups in the US chart, the Korean chart includes a section for sugar and oil. This section is, of course, the smallest.

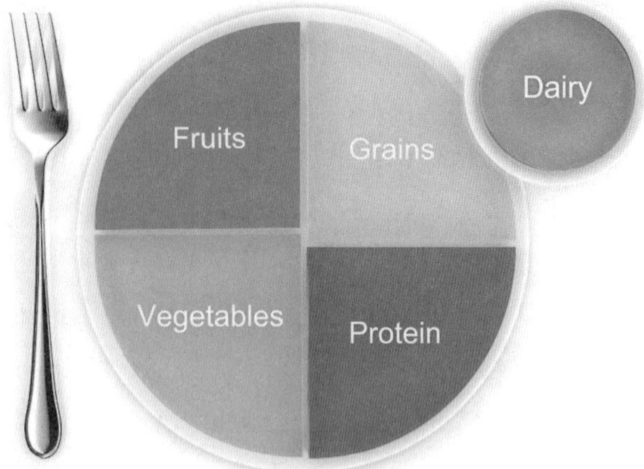

▲ United States food balance chart

Brazil's food guide doesn't have food groups like vegetables or dairy. It says to eat more unprocessed food, less processed food, and no ultra-processed food. Take fish as an example. Fresh fish is unprocessed. It's healthy. Canned fish is processed. It's not as good for you as fresh fish. Finally, frozen fish nuggets are ultra-processed. Ultra-processed foods are not healthy because they have a lot of **artificial** ingredients and **preservatives**. The message is that unprocessed food is better for you.

grains rice, bread, oatmeal, etc.
artificial man-made, not natural
preservatives something put in food to make it last longer

A Read the article. Circle **T** for *true* or **F** for *false*.

1. Some countries give information to help people make good food choices.	T	F
2. The countries in the article are the US, Korea, and Brazil.	T	F
3. The US chart is a triangle.	T	F
4. The US chart says you only need a little milk or yogurt.	T	F
5. The Korean chart includes coffee and tea.	T	F
6. Brazil's food groups are the same as Korea's.	T	F
7. Unprocessed food has chemicals and preservatives.	T	F
8. Natural or unprocessed food is good for you.	T	F

B Write the food groups in order from the food you need a lot of (1) to the food you only need a little of (3).

dairy fruits and protein vegetables and grains

1. ______________________

2. ______________________

3. ______________________

C Answer the questions.

1. What foods are in the protein group? Give two examples. ______________________

2. How many food groups does Korea's chart have? ______________________

3. What groups are on the Korean chart and not on the US chart? ______________________

4. How many food groups are in Brazil's food guide? ______________________

5. What are Brazil's food groups? ______________________

6. In Brazil, fresh vegetables are an example of which food group? ______________________

7. In Brazil, a bag of potato chips is an example of which food group? ______________________

D Which country's food information do you think is the most helpful? Why?

____

____

____

____

____

Lesson E Writing

A Complete the paragraph with the sequencing words.

after that finally first meanwhile next then

(1) ______________, check that you have all of the ingredients that you need.

(2) ______________, put all of the ingredients on the table or counter. (3) ______________, read the recipe again to be sure you understand all of the steps. (4) ______________, follow the recipe and start making the food. (5) ______________, turn on the oven to heat it up. (6) ______________, put the food in the oven and set the timer.

B Look at the picture of a maze. Complete the instructions for going through it. Remember to add commas.

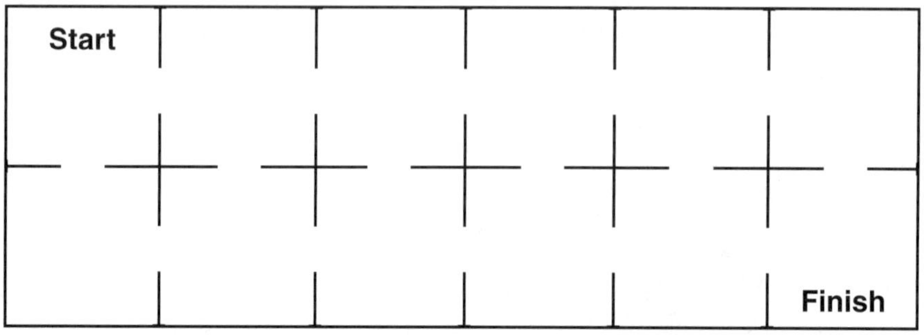

1. ______________ stand with your back and your left side to the walls that are not open.
2. ______________ walk straight into the next room and the one after that.
3. ______________ turn right and walk into the next room.
4. ______________ turn left and walk straight through two rooms.
5. ______________ continue straight to the last room. You made it to the end!

C Use the maze in **B** to write new instructions to go from start to finish. Include at least six steps.

____

____

____

____

D Imagine that you are helping a friend who wants to send a text message with a photo on a smartphone, but doesn't know how. Explain the instructions for using your phone to send a photo. Include at least six steps.

____

____

____

____

____

Review

A Circle the correct word. Choose *x* if no word is needed.

1. Would you like *a* / *an* / *x* orange?
2. She eats *a* / *an* / *x* chicken sandwich for lunch every Monday.
3. There is *a* / *an* / *x* butter in the fridge.
4. Do you drink *a* / *an* / *x* soda?
5. Please buy *a* / *an* / *x* bag of potatoes at the store.

B 14 Listen and complete the conversation.

1. **A:** This potato salad is good. What are the ingredients?
   B: It is very simple. _______ potatoes, _______ onion, _______ mayonnaise, and _______ salt and pepper.
   A: Do you put _______ blue cheese on it?
   B: No, I usually don't. Would you like _______?
2. **A:** I want _______ BLT sandwich for lunch.
   B: What's _______ BLT?
   A: It's _______ sandwich with bacon, lettuce, and tomato.
   B: Oh, I see. Do you have the ingredients?
   A: Well, there are _______ tomatoes on the table and there is _______ lettuce in the fridge.
   B: Do you have _______ turkey bacon?
   A: I don't see _______ in the fridge. And I don't have _______ bread, either.
   B: Then let's go out to lunch. You can order a BLT at the restaurant!

C Find the error in each sentence. Rewrite the sentence so it is correct.

1. How many orange juice do you need? ____________________
2. He drinks a little of coffee in the morning. Sometimes five cups! ____________________
3. There is not many sugar in the sugar bowl. ____________________
4. Don't buy tomatoes. We have lot of home grown ones. ____________________
5. My son likes a few of vegetables with his dinner. ____________________
6. How much apples do you need to make apple pie? ____________________

Video A Guerilla Gardener in South Central LA

A Answer the questions.

1. Do you have a garden? Do your friends or neighbors?
____
2. Do you eat fresh vegetables? If you do, where do they come from?
____
3. Do you think it's hard work to have a garden? Why?
____

B Watch the video. Write the word(s) from the box that mean(s) the same as the underlined word(s).

is therapeutic	maintains	opportunity	sustainable	volunteers

1. The city owns the land, but Ron Finley <u>takes care of</u> it. ______________
2. The people who plant the gardens are <u>not paid</u>. ______________
3. Gardening <u>makes you feel better</u>. ______________
4. Finley thinks gardening is a good <u>chance</u> for kids. ______________
5. Growing your own food is <u>something you can do for a long time</u>. ______________

C Watch the video again. Read the statements. Do you think Ron Finley agrees or disagrees? Write *A* (agrees) or *D* (disagrees).

______ **1.** The LA Green Grounds group works hard.
______ **2.** Gardening is good for you and your community.
______ **3.** Growing food is a good way to make money.
______ **4.** Gardens can change communities.
______ **5.** The garden in front of my house isn't only for me.
______ **6.** Growing food doesn't help kids eat more vegetables.
______ **7.** A garden is something to be proud of.

D Ron Finley says kids are proud of the garden. What is something that you are proud of? Is it something you do in a group or on your own?

____
____
____
____

Sports

UNIT 5

Lesson A Vocabulary and Grammar

A Look at the pictures. Write questions and answers with the present continuous.

1. 

a. What is he doing?

b. He's snowboarding.

2. 

a. ______________________

b. ______________________

3. 

a. ______________________

b. ______________________

4. 

a. ______________________

b. ______________________

5. 

a. ______________________

b. ______________________

6. 

a. ______________________

b. ______________________

B Complete the sentences with the present continuous.

1. My brother ______________________ (play) tennis with our cousin.
2. What movie ______________________ (they / watch) on TV?
3. The students ______________________ (take) a test in the classroom.
4. Mina and Jiwoom ______________________ (jog) in their neighborhood.
5. What kind of music ______________________ (you / listen) to?
6. Where ______________________ (we / go) today?

C Today is a holiday. Look at these people's activities and, in your notebook, write sentences with the simple present and present continuous.

	Mondays	Today, Monday May 1st
Nadia	clean her house	watch a movie
Javier	go to his office	sleep late
Ms. Tyson	teach classes	swim at the sports center
Yuki and Yoko	study English	hike with friends
Mr. Kim	drive a bus	cook for his family

(Nadia) On Mondays, Nadia usually cleans her house. Today, she is watching a movie.

Lesson B Listening

A 15 Listen to the sentences. Are the speakers talking about things they usually do or things they're doing right now? Circle the correct answer.

1. usually right now
2. usually right now
3. usually right now
4. usually right now
5. usually right now
6. usually right now
7. usually right now

B 16 Listen to the conversations. Read the sentences. Then circle **T** for *true* or **F** for *false*.

1. Saruka is going to the beach with her friends. T F
2. Diego and his brother usually go to the movies on Saturday afternoon. T F
3. Diego likes to sit in the sun at the beach. T F
4. Diego is going to talk to his brother about going to the beach. T F
5. Niko usually studies on Sundays. T F
6. Haruto is visiting Niko this weekend. T F
7. Haruto's cousins usually visit him on the weekends. T F
8. Niko isn't going ice skating. T F

C Match the questions to the answers.

_______ **1.** Do you walk home from class?
_______ **2.** Do you often go swimming in the summer?
_______ **3.** What are you buying?
_______ **4.** Do you call your parents every week?
_______ **5.** What do you do?
_______ **6.** Are you studying right now?
_______ **7.** Are you watching the basketball game on TV?

a. Yes. And we text a few times a week.
b. Yes, I am. I'm in the library.
c. A pair of jeans and a shirt.
d. Sometimes, but I usually take the bus.
e. Yes, I do. I live close to the beach.
f. No, I'm not.
g. I'm a student.

Lesson C Vocabulary and Grammar

A Write the name of the activity Then write T (team) or I (individual).

1. ____________

2. ____________

3. ____________

4. ____________

5. ____________

6. ____________

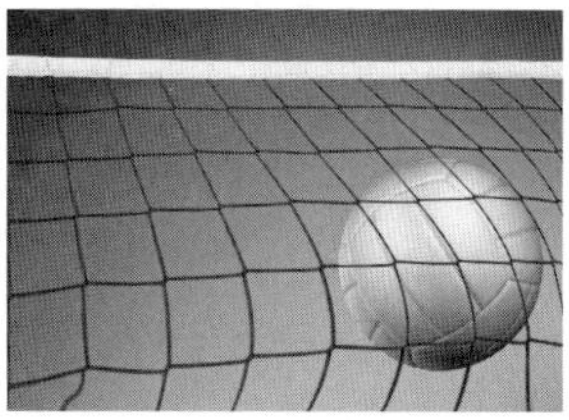

7. ____________

8. ____________

B 17 Read the phone conversation. Write the correct form of the verb in parentheses—simple present or present continuous. Then listen and check your answers.

Amy: Hi, Yoshi. What (1) __are you doing__ (you, do)? It's very noisy there.

Yoshi: I (2) ____________ (watch) a football game at the stadium! It's American football.

Amy: Really? (3) ____________ (you, like) it?

Yoshi: Yes! But I (4) ____________ (know, not) very much about the sport. All the players (5) ____________ (run), and one player (6) ____________ (throw) the ball.

Amy: And all the people (7) ____________ (shout)!

Yoshi: You should come to a game with me. The tickets only (8) ____________ (cost) $5.

Amy: I (9) ____________ (want, not) to watch football. I (10) ____________ (hate) team sports. I (11) ____________ (prefer) individual sports like swimming and running.

Yoshi: What (12) ____________ (you, do) today?

Amy: Right now, I (13) ____________ (go) to the pool for a swim.

C Unscramble the words to make sentences.

1. players / does / how many / need / a baseball team ____________
2. cold days / hates / very / skiing / she / on ____________
3. does / why / prefer / individual / he / sports ____________
4. thinks / is / rock climbing / Natalia / dangerous ____________
5. volleyball / how to / play / know / you / do ____________
6. game / he / the / Real Madrid / to win / wants / soccer ____________

Capoeira

Capoeira is a martial art from Brazil. A martial art is a type of sport that is a form of self-defense. Karate and judo are other examples of popular martial arts.

Capoeira looks like a mix of fighting and dancing. It is a fast sport because the people doing capoeira, often called "players," need to stay **in motion**. Each player moves to make it difficult for the other person to kick or hit them. Players need strong legs because kicking is a big part of the sport. Players usually attack with their legs, not their arms. Sometimes one person falls to the floor. But the goal of capoeira is not to hurt the other player.

Capoeira is all about skill. Players need to avoid the opponent's attacks. Also, they need to confuse or trick the other player. Some moves make a player think their opponent will move one way, but they move the other way.

Capoeira players are sometimes called *capoeiristas*. Two capoeiristas practice within a large circle of people who usually sing and clap while they watch. Often, there is music playing to help the capoeiristas keep in motion. People do capoeira indoors and outdoors. The players don't need any equipment. They usually wear a white T-shirt and loose white pants. The T-shirts often have the name of the players' clubs on them. Many players don't wear shoes. Those who do need lightweight shoes with a good grip on the **sole**.

in motion moving
sole the bottom of a shoe

Capoeiristas practicing on a beach

A Read the article. Circle **T** for *true* or **F** for *false*.

1. Capoeira is a martial art from Japan.	T	F
2. Players must move without stopping.	T	F
3. Players usually attack with their head and arms.	T	F
4. The first player to fall loses the game.	T	F
5. Players must try to confuse their opponent.	T	F
6. Capoeira is a team sport.	T	F
7. Capoeira is only an indoor sport.	T	F
8. Players don't need to wear shoes.	T	F

B Match these words from the text with the correct definition.

_______ **1.** self-defense **a.** try to hit someone

_______ **2.** skill **b.** confuse someone

_______ **3.** opponent **c.** protecting yourself from something

_______ **4.** attack **d.** the ability to do something well

_______ **5.** trick **e.** the person or team you play against

C Complete the sentences with the words in the box. Two words can't be used.

circle	clap	dance	hurt	kick	loose	moving	music	shoes	trick

1. Capoeira players don't stop _______________.

2. Players need strong legs to _______________ hard.

3. Players try to _______________ one another.

4. The game is played inside a _______________.

5. People who watch the game sing and _______________.

6. _______________ helps the players keep moving.

7. Players usually wear _______________ white pants and a T-shirt.

8. Not all players wear _______________.

D Answer the questions.

1. How is capoeira like dancing? _______________

2. How is it like fighting? _______________

3. Do you think you would like to try capoeira? Why? _______________

A Complete the questions with the words from the box. You can use one option more than once.

Do	Do you	How many	How often	What	When	Would

1. ________________ watch sports on TV?
2. ________________ do you watch sports on TV?
3. ________________ do you normally watch sports on TV?
4. ________________ sports do you watch?
5. ________________ hours do you watch TV each weekend?
6. ________________ channel do you usually watch?
7. ________________ you recommend that channel to your friends?
8. ________________ you go to basketball games?

B Which questions in **A** are open and which are closed? Write the numbers.

Open: ________________

Closed: ________________

C Imagine that your school is having yoga classes to help students relax. Complete the questionnaire with your own ideas.

Please take a few minutes to answer these questions about our yoga classes.

1. Do you go to the yoga classes? ☐ Yes ☐ No
2. How often do you go to the yoga classes? ☐ 1–2 times a week ☐ 3–5 times a week ☐ Never
3. When do you normally go to the yoga classes? ☐ Before class ☐ At lunchtime ☐ After class
4. Why do you go to the yoga classes? ☐ To stay in shape ☐ To meet people ☐ To relax
5. Do the yoga classes help you to relax? ☐ Yes ☐ No

D Write a questionnaire about a sporting event, such as a soccer or basketball game. Write at least six questions. Some possible topics are ticket prices, refreshments, restrooms, game times, etc.

____

____

____

____

____

____

Review

A Unscramble the words to write questions.

1. are / watching / where / the game / you ______________________________?
2. are / with / their / friends / English / speaking / they ______________________________?
3. tea / you / coffee / are / drinking / or ______________________________?
4. climbing / is / without / he / ropes ______________________________?
5. buying / supermarket / are / the / you / at / what ______________________________?
6. she / teacher / why / the / to / talking / is ______________________________?

B Circle the correct verb form to complete the sentences.

1. Monica *listens* / *is listening* to music in the mornings.
2. Reo and Itsuki *climb* / *are climbing* the most dangerous part of the mountain today.
3. They *study* / *are studying* right now.
4. This morning they *play* / *are playing* tennis at the courts in the park.
5. The children *don't swim* / *aren't swimming* in the pool today.
6. He *jogs* / *is jogging* every morning before work.
7. She *hikes* / *is hiking* in Peru with three friends.

C Complete the sentences with the correct forms of the verbs in the box.

cost	hate	know	like	look	prefer	think	want

1. Marco doesn't ______________ to watch sports.
2. Her friends snowboard, but she ______________ skiing.
3. We ______________ rock climbing is dangerous.
4. The volleyball team ______________ to lose.
5. I don't ______________ how to play tennis.
6. Skateboarding ______________ difficult.
7. A membership there ______________ a lot of money.
8. Mei ______________ to be a gymnast.

D Complete the sentences with the correct form of *do*, *go*, or *play*.

1. Does Rafael ______________ soccer for his school's team?
2. Beatriz is in the gym ______________ gymnastics.
3. They often ______________ skiing in the winter.
4. Diem usually ______________ jogging after work.
5. How many times a week do you ______________ yoga?
6. Luiz ______________ baseball on Thursday evenings.

Video Free Soloing with Alex Honnold

A Look at the picture. What sport is this? Do you think it is a safe activity? Why?

____

B Watch the video. Read the sentences. Circle **T** for *true* or **F** for *false*.

1. Free soloing is a team sport.	T	F
2. Alex wants to free solo to the top of Half Dome.	T	F
3. Half Dome is a popular place for climbing because it's easy.	T	F
4. Alex thinks about the climb a lot before he starts.	T	F
5. He doesn't need a lot of equipment.	T	F
6. He eats breakfast with a spoon.	T	F
7. He climbs quickly.	T	F
8. He stops to rest and think about what he's doing.	T	F

▲ Alex Honnold on Half Dome in Yosemite National Park, California, USA

C Complete the sentences from the video with the correct stative verbs.

1. "Sometimes he climbs with ropes, but he ______________ free soloing because he can move more quickly."
2. "Alex ______________ to climb up a vertical wall called Half Dome."
3. "But Alex ______________ to climb the wall without ropes."
4. "He ______________ a good breakfast."
5. "He ______________ every part of the wall and he continues to climb."

D Answer the questions with your own ideas. Explain your answers.

1. Do you think free soloing is a popular sport? Why? ______________________________

____

2. Is free soloing a sport you want to try? Why? ______________________________

____

3. Imagine a close friend or family member tells you they want to try a dangerous sport. What advice do you give them? ______________________________

____

____

____

____

Destinations

Lesson A Vocabulary and Grammar

A Complete the sentences with the simple past form of a verb from the box. Two verbs can't be used.

buy	do	eat	fly	go	pack	rent	see	stay	take

1. We ____________ photos of Machu Picchu.
2. I ____________ the local food in Vietnam and I liked it!
3. They ____________ so many famous places on their trip to Europe.
4. My parents ____________ a car when they visited me.
5. ____________ you change money at the airport?
6. Juana ____________ souvenirs at the market.
7. He ____________ with a friend in Kyoto.
8. Ting ____________ one small suitcase for the weekend.

B Write the simple past form of the verb. Some verbs are regular and some are irregular.

ask		leave	
buy		need	
eat		play	*played*
fly		say	
go		see	
help		take	*took*
know		tell	
learn		travel	

C Complete the sentences with the correct verb.

1. Marisol and Javier ______ Lima on Saturday.
   a. arrived **b.** left **c.** stayed
2. They ______ to Cusco.
   a. flew **b.** visited **c.** left
3. The flight ______ about an hour and a half long.
   a. was **b.** are **c.** went
4. In Cusco, they ______ a taxi from the airport to the hotel.
   a. went **b.** rented **c.** took
5. They ______ to the hotel and unpacked their suitcases.
   a. stayed **b.** checked in **c.** changed in
6. On Sunday, they ______ some famous places in Cusco.
   a. spent **b.** went **c.** saw

Lesson B Listening

A Two people are talking about a vacation. Write the questions.

1. **Q:** ______________________________?
   A: I went to Buenos Aires, in Argentina.
2. **Q:** ______________________________?
   A: I stayed there for a week.
3. **Q:** ______________________________?
   A: I visited some famous places and ate great food.
4. **Q:** ______________________________?
   A: I bought a new jacket.
5. **Q:** ______________________________?
   A: Yes, I really enjoyed it! It's a beautiful city!

B 19 Complete the conversation. Use the words in parentheses to write questions and answers in the simple past. Then listen and check your answers.

Andres: Tell me about your vacation, Magaly. (1) ____________________ (where / go)?

Magaly: (2) ____________________ (we / go / to India). It was great!

Andres: (3) ____________________ (where / fly to)?

Magaly: (4) ____________________ (fly / to New Delhi). We stayed for two nights.

(5) ____________________ (then / we / take / a train to Agra).

Andres: (6) ____________________ (what / do in Agra)?

Magaly: (7) ____________________ (we / visit / the Taj Mahal). It was beautiful!

Andres: What about the food in India? (8) ____________________ (you / like it)?

Magaly: Yes! (9) ____________________ (we / go) to some great restaurants.

C 20 Listen to the conversation. Read the sentences. Then circle **T** for *true* or **F** for *false*.

1. Fumiko and Emilio are talking about a long weekend.	T	F
2. Fumiko went on a cruise with her family.	T	F
3. First, they flew to Mexico.	T	F
4. They spent the whole time on the cruise ship.	T	F
5. Fumiko visited a city called Merida.	T	F
6. They saw ancient ruins.	T	F
7. Emilio asked how long they were on the cruise.	T	F
8. Fumiko ate a very hot pepper.	T	F

Lesson C Vocabulary and Grammar

A Matias and Jorge are traveling together. Matias uses simple adjectives, but Jorge prefers emphatic adjectives. Write Jorge's sentences with words from the box.

awful	exhausting	fascinating	filthy
huge	outstanding	spotless	

Matias	**Jorge**
1. The food was good.	The food was outstanding.
2. The hotel rooms were clean.	______
3. The 12-hour flight was tiring.	______
4. The subway was dirty.	______
5. The traffic was bad.	______
6. The guided tour was interesting.	______
7. My backpack was big.	______

B Circle the correct form of *be* to complete the sentence.

1. How *was* / *wasn't* / *were* your vacation?
2. The mountains *was* / *wasn't* / *were* enormous.
3. Their trip to Costa Rica *was* / *weren't* / *were* amazing.
4. What *was* / *wasn't* / *were* the two best things about your trip?
5. We walked around the city all day. We *were* / *weren't* / *was* exhausted in the evening.
6. The guided tours *weren't* / *wasn't* / *was* very interesting. I *were* / *was* / *wasn't* bored.

C Use the words to write statements and questions with the simple past of *be*.

1. how / be / your / camping trip How was your camping trip?
2. be / the guided tours / expensive ______
3. the food / in / our hotel / not be / very good ______
4. the art museum / be / huge ______
5. the rental car / not be / too / expensive ______
6. what / be / your favorite / attraction ______

D Complete the sentences with *was*, *were*, *wasn't*, or *weren't*.

My weekend (1) ______ fun. I went to the beach with friends. The weather was great. It (2) ______ hot and sunny. The beach was crowded. There (3) ______ a lot of people there. The water (4) ______ very warm, but we swam anyway. For lunch, we bought sandwiches at the snack bar, but they (5) ______ very good. So we ate ice cream instead. We saw some people playing soccer on the beach, so we joined them. They (6) ______ good players. I (7) ______ exhausted when I got home!

Giants on a Small Island

Rapa Nui, or Easter Island, is a small island in the Pacific Ocean. This little island is famous for some very old and very large statues. These statues, called *moai*, are hundreds of years old. They are enormous. The largest is 33 feet tall and weighs 80 tons. Even the smallest statue is big—it's 4 feet tall.

About a thousand years ago, people sailed from Polynesia to Rapa Nui. They settled on the island and made the statues from volcanic rock. They made eyes from white coral and used a black or red stone for the **pupil**. Some statues have headpieces, which could be hair or hats, made from red volcanic rock.

Researchers say the statues probably honor the **ancestors** of the Polynesian settlers. Rapanui legend says the statues have their ancestors' spirits inside them. There are many different ideas about how the statues came to be standing up.

The statues are located all over the island, usually close to the water. The rock used to make the statues came from miles away from where they stand. How did people move huge, heavy statues hundreds of years ago? Rapanui legend says they walked, and that the spirits of powerful ancestors inside the statues made it happen.

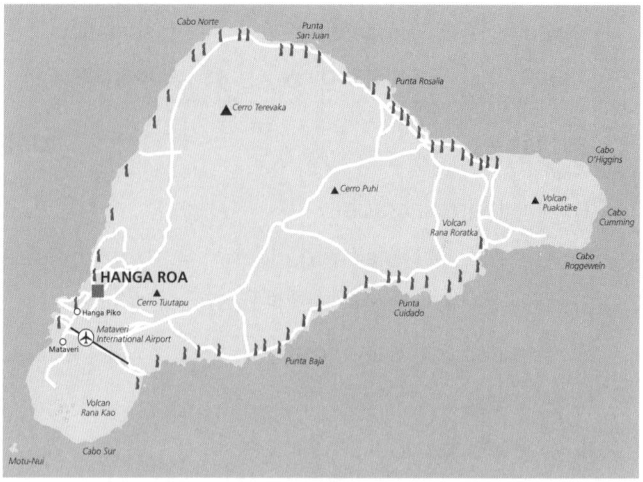

▲ The black figures show the locations of the statues.

Researchers have different ideas about how the statues moved. Some think that people rolled the statues using cut wood. Other researchers think that people pulled and rolled the statues on to their rounded front sides. In fact, research teams have tried to recreate moving artificial statues to test their ideas. They were able to move the statues, but they were exhausted from the hard work.

pupil the dark circle in the middle of the eye
ancestor a person in your family who lived a long time ago

Moai statues on Easter Island

A Read the article. Match the sentence parts.

______	**1.** Rapa Nui is also called	**a.**	white coral and stones.
______	**2.** *Moai* are the	**b.**	volcanic rock.
______	**3.** The people on Rapa Nui came from	**c.**	Polynesia.
______	**4.** The eyes were made from	**d.**	Easter Island.
______	**5.** The statues are made of	**e.**	statues walked.
______	**6.** Rapanui legend says the	**f.**	statues.

B Read the article again. Circle **T** for *true* or **F** for *false*.

1.	Most of the *moai* statues are taller than a person.	T	F
2.	The statues are more than 1,000 years old.	T	F
3.	The settlers probably carved the statues to honor people who lived before them.	T	F
4.	Researchers say the statues have spirits inside them.	T	F
5.	All of the statues are close to the water.	T	F
6.	The statues were rolled down a mountain to the beaches.	T	F
7.	Researchers disagree about how people moved the statues.	T	F

C Complete the sentences with a word from the box.

artificial	coral	legend	Polynesia	researcher	ton

1. A ____________________ is about 900 kilograms.

2. ____________________ is a name for a group of islands in the Pacific Ocean.

3. ____________________ is made of tiny sea animal bones.

4. A ____________________ is an old story told again and again.

5. Something that is ____________________ is not real.

6. A ____________________ studies something to learn new things.

D Answer the questions about the article in complete sentences.

1. What are two facts about the *moai* statues? ______________________________

____

2. What do the statues look like? ______________________________

____

3. What are two ideas about how the statues came to stand up? ______________________________

____

____

____

Lesson E Writing

A Complete the sentences with the correct time references.

1. _______ was the last day of my vacation.

a. Yesterday **b.** On January 1st,

2. Hana began to study English _______ and now she is an English teacher.

a. this morning **b.** in 2016

3. _______ I was afraid to speak in class.

a. In 2001, **b.** When I was a student,

4. _______ my friend arrived from Cartagena.

a. When I was young, **b.** The day before yesterday,

5. _______ technology changed quickly.

a. A year ago, **b.** During the 20th century,

6. Reo was a student in Tokyo _______.

a. between 2015 and 2017 **b.** last night

7. She was late for class _______.

a. last year **b.** this morning

8. Manuel learned to drive _______.

a. on September 3rd **b.** last year

B Complete the sentences with time references.

1. The first time I flew in an airplane was _______________.

2. _______________ I met my best friend.

3. _______________ I started to study English.

4. _______________ cell phones became popular in my country.

5. I visited _______________ for the first time _______________.

6. _______________ I watched TV.

7. I ate breakfast _______________.

C Read the blog post by a student. Underline the time references and circle the verbs in the simple past.

English-language-learner. Posted by milagros, April 8, 9:40 p.m.

Hi, my name's Milagros. I started studying English in 2016. I was a high school student. My English class was not difficult, but I didn't speak well. A year ago, I started classes with a tutor. This helped me with conversation skills. I learned new words and grammar in conversation before I learned to read and write them. This way of learning worked for me. Between 2016 and 2018, I continued to learn English in school, but the extra practice with a tutor was important for me. After high school, I went to college, where I met a lot of people who spoke English. Talking to friends and classmates in English helped me improve quickly. I spoke better and understood more. Now I feel confident about my English.

D In your notebook, write about your experience learning English for a blog for other students. Use time references and the simple past.

Review

A Complete the sentences with the emphatic adjectives from the box. Use each word once.

exhausting	filthy	horrible	huge	spotless

1. The food in the restaurant was bad. In fact, I thought it was ________________.
2. My hotel room was very clean. In fact, it was ________________.
3. The trip was really tiring. In fact, it was ________________.
4. The beaches were very dirty. In fact, they were ________________.
5. The store was very big. In fact, it was ________________.

B Read the tour schedule. Imagine you took the tour. Write sentences in the simple past.

A Week in Rio de Janeiro!

Monday	Leave home and fly to Rio. Go to the hotel.
Tuesday	Visit the Botanical Gardens and Maracana stadium.
Wednesday	Take a cable car to the top of Sugarloaf Mountain.
Thursday	See a capoeira performance and go to a bossa nova concert.
Friday	Relax at Ipanema and Copacabana beaches.
Saturday	Go shopping at an outdoor market and buy souvenirs.
Sunday	Go to the airport. Go home.

1. *On Monday, I left home and flew to Rio de Janeiro. I went to my hotel.*
2. ________________________________
3. ________________________________
4. ________________________________
5. ________________________________
6. ________________________________
7. ________________________________

C Complete the sentences with *was*, *wasn't*, *were*, and *weren't*.

1. Jacob ________________ in class yesterday because he ________________ sick.
2. The stores ________________ open last Monday because it ________________ a holiday.
3. I didn't enjoy my vacation. The hotel ________________ horrible, and the restaurants ________________ expensive.
4. I got 90 percent on the test. It ________________ very long, and the questions ________________ easy.
5. Where ________________ you last night? I called you, but your phone ________________ turned off.

Video Vietnam's Green Jewels

A Read and answer the questions.

1. Where is Vietnam? Describe its location on the map.

____

____

2. What is a bay? Is there a bay in your area? If yes, what is its name?

____

____

3. Have you visited a small island? If yes, what was it like?

____

____

B Match the words to the meanings.

_____ **1.** region	**a.** a beautiful stone
_____ **2.** uninhabited by humans	**b.** animals that live in natural places
_____ **3.** wildlife	**c.** the huge rocks in the bay
_____ **4.** legend	**d.** an area of land
_____ **5.** jewel	**e.** people do not live there
_____ **6.** karsts	**f.** a very old story

C Watch the video. Complete the sentences with the numbers in the video.

1. "There are around ____________ islands covering an area of ____________ square kilometers."
2. "____________ of tourists visit the region every day."
3. "____________ of boats sail around the islands every day."
4. "Created over ____________ of years, they are between ____________ and ____________ feet tall."
5. "There are ____________ national parks."
6. "Ha Long Bay has around ____________ visitors a year."

D Imagine you are a tour guide in Ha Long Bay. Do you tell the tourists about the dragon legend, the scientific history of the bay, or both? Why?

____

____

____

____

____

____

Communication

Lesson A Vocabulary and Grammar

A Unscramble the ways to communicate.

1. ileam ______________________
2. xtte ssamege __________ __________
3. loicas damei __________ __________
4. idvoe smaegse __________ __________
5. cesarh gnniee __________ __________
6. mthaorpsen ______________________
7. meag sonolce __________ __________

B Write the things in **A** that you use. Include who you use them with.

____

____

____

C Complete the sentences with indirect objects. Use object pronouns (*me*, *you*, *him*, *her*, *it*, *us*, *them*).

1. I'm hungry. Please give __________ a sandwich.
2. It's her birthday. You should buy __________ a present.
3. I don't know their phone number. I'll send __________ an email.
4. My grandfather lives in Mexico, but I send __________ text messages all the time.
5. The dog is thirsty. Please give __________ some water.
6. You look bored. I'll tell __________ an interesting story.
7. We want to talk to you. Please give __________ a call.

D Look at the pictures and write requests or descriptions. Use direct and indirect objects.

1. 

Please give me a call.

She gives him a call.

2. 

____

____

3. 

____

____

4. 

____

____

5. 

____

____

6. 

____

____

A 22 Write the numbers you hear in words.

1. ______________ 7. ______________
2. ______________ 8. ______________
3. ______________ 9. ______________
4. ______________ 10. ______________
5. ______________ 11. ______________
6. ______________ 12. ______________

B Complete the sentences with words from the box.

email address	mailing address	phone number	social media

1. My ______________ is rita at coolmail dot com.
2. My ______________ is area code eight-one-eight, five-five-five, nine-oh-one-two.
3. My ______________ is four-thirty-three Russell Road, Middletown, zip code four-eight-seven-two-eight.
4. Follow me on ______________ at rita seven two four.

REAL LANGUAGE

People "follow" each other on social media by finding a person's name, or handle, on the website. The symbol @ is pronounced "at" and is common on many social media websites.

C Complete the address book. Write the information in words.

You	Your friend	Your family member
Name: ______________	Name: ______________	Name: ______________
1. My phone number is ______________ ______________	**1.** His/Her phone number is ______________ ______________	**1.** His/Her phone number is ______________ ______________
2. Follow me: ______________ ______________	**2.** Follow him/her: ______________ ______________	**2.** Follow him/her: ______________ ______________
3. My mailing address is ______________ ______________ ______________ ______________	**3.** His/Her mailing address is ______________ ______________ ______________ ______________	**3.** His/Her mailing address is ______________ ______________ ______________ ______________
4. My email address is ______________ ______________	**4.** His/Her email address is ______________ ______________	**4.** His/Her email address is ______________ ______________

Lesson C Vocabulary and Grammar

A Label the pictures with the correct senses from the box.

hearing sight smell taste touch

1. ______________ **2.** ______________ **3.** ______________ **4.** ______________ **5.** ______________

B Match the sentence parts.

_______ **1.** That fish is old. It smells

_______ **2.** I like this jacket because it feels so

_______ **3.** I don't like potato chips. They taste too

_______ **4.** I went out in the rain. Now my clothes feel

_______ **5.** Don't wear those jeans. They look

_______ **6.** My brother plays the drums. They sound very

_______ **7.** You shouldn't eat those bananas. They look too

_______ **8.** I love chocolate because it tastes

a. sweet.
b. loud.
c. soft.
d. salty.
e. wet.
f. dirty.
g. bad.
h. green.

C Circle the correct verb.

1. Can you hear that? My computer *sounds* / *looks* strange.
2. I like Thai food because it *feels* / *tastes* spicy.
3. Your new sunglasses *look* / *taste* really cool. Where did you get them?
4. My friend gave me some perfume. It *looks* / *smells* like flowers.
5. The water *feels* / *sounds* really cold. I don't want to go swimming.
6. That camera *sounds* / *looks* expensive. How much does it cost?

D Complete the sentences. Use your own ideas.

1. (taste) I like ______________________ because it tastes ______________________.
2. (smell) I don't like ______________________ because ______________________.
3. (feel) ____.
4. (look) ____.
5. (sound) ____.

How Do Animals Communicate?

Animals communicate in many different ways. Some animals use their whole bodies. For example, bees dance to communicate. They send messages about flowers and other places with food. Other bees see the dance and find the food.

Some insects communicate with smells. They produce chemicals so that other insects can find them. Wolves and dogs also use smell to get a lot of information about other animals. And cats like to rub their bodies on things like trees to put their smell on them. The smell means, "This tree is mine!"

Many animals communicate by touching. For example, chimpanzees say "hello" by touching another chimpanzee's hand. When two horses put their noses together, it means, "We are friends."

And, of course, many animals communicate with sounds. Birds use their beautiful songs to communicate. Dogs, cats, and people all make different kinds of sounds to send many different messages.

▲ a chimpanzee

▲ a bee

▲ a wolf

▲ an insect

A Write the names of the animals next to the sense(s) they use to communicate.

bee bird cat chimpanzee dog horse wolf

Hearing	
Sight	
Smell	
Touch	

B Complete the sentences.

1. Bees dance to tell other bees about ______________________.
2. Insects use ______________________ to find other insects.
3. ______________________ like to put their smell on things.
4. Horses use their noses to communicate that they are ______________________.
5. People and birds both use ______________________ to communicate.

C Match the animal communication with its meaning.

_______ 1. A dog wags (moves) its tail.
_______ 2. A cat wags its tail.
_______ 3. A skunk lifts its tail.
_______ 4. A snake moves its tail and makes a noise.

a. It is angry.
b. Stay away—it can bite.
c. It is happy.
d. Stay away—it smells.

▲ a skunk

A Write about the ways you communicate with your friends. What do you use to communicate? When is your communication formal and when is it informal?

____

____

____

____

____

B Look at the diagram below. How did Sanjay hear the news? Write sentences with indirect objects. (In 1–5, write each sentence two different ways.)

Tara sent an email	→	Brian sent a text message	→	Daniel wrote a letter	→	Sophia told Melanie the news	→	Melanie gave a phone call	→	Sanjay heard the news!

1. a. Tara sent Brian an email.
   b. Tara sent an email to Brian.
2. a. ______________________
   b. ______________________
3. a. ______________________
   b. ______________________
4. a. ______________________
   b. ______________________
5. a. ______________________
   b. ______________________

C Ask another student questions about the sentences above. How did each person get the news?

How did Brian get the news?

Tara sent him an email.

D Write a paragraph with the title: *How Sanjay heard the news.* Use these sequence words: *First, Next, Then, After that, Finally.*

____

____

____

____

____

____

____

Review

A Solve the crossword puzzle with vocabulary and grammar from this unit.

Across

5. simple past of *buy*
7. I wrote him a short _______ message.
8. French fries _______ salty.
10. Drums _______ loud.
12. I wrote to my mother. I sent _______ a letter.
14. I made a _______ call.
15. Those photos _______ interesting.

Down

1. simple past of *send*
2. simple past of *write*
3. simple past of *find*
4. simple past of *get*
6. This sense uses your ears.
9. This sense uses your hands.
10. Flowers _______ sweet.
11. This sense uses your eyes.
13. These sweaters _______ soft.

B Complete the text with words from the box.

~~communicate~~	email	smartphone	social media	text message

We (1) ___communicate___ in many different ways. Most people have a cell phone or a computer. With a cell phone, you can communicate quickly with a call or a (2) _______________, and with your computer and the internet, you can send an (3) _______________. Nowadays, more and more people are using (4) _______________ to communicate with their family and friends and to share information and photos. It's a fast way to be in contact with a lot of people at the same time. If you have a (5) _______________, you can make calls, send text messages and emails, and communicate via social media—all from one device!

Video A New View of the Moon

A Watch the video. Then unscramble the sentences.

want to / look / the / you / at / do / moon

(1) ____

where / look / supposed to / am / I

(2) ____

right / supposed to / you / look / are / here

(3) ____

the / I / at / moon / looking / am

(4) ____

it / of / want / more / I / see / to

(5) ____

B Some people in the video think what they see is interesting. Write about four times you saw, tasted, smelled or felt something interesting. Use a different word from the box in each sentence.

amazing	awesome	fantastic	incredible

1. ____
____.

2. ____
____.

3. ____
____.

4. ____
____.

Making Plans

UNIT 8

Lesson A Vocabulary and Grammar

A Complete the sentences with the correct form of a verb in the box. You can use some words more than once.

buy	clean	do	get	have	speak	study	take

1. Maria is ______________ the house.
2. Isabel and Ken are ______________ married soon.
3. Are you ______________ for the test?
4. Riko's long-term plan is to ______________ English fluently.
5. Jakob needs to ______________ a new job.
6. My parents are ______________ a new house.
7. Mr. Natzuke is ______________ a vacation this week.
8. Jorge is ______________ the laundry.
9. Jihoo and Mina want to ______________ children.
10. Leticia wants to ______________ a new car.

B Match the questions and answers.

______ **1.** Is he buying a new car?
______ **2.** Is Anita doing the laundry today?
______ **3.** Are you taking a vacation soon?
______ **4.** Is Yasmin getting a new job?
______ **5.** Do you want to buy your own house?
______ **6.** Are you and your partner going to get married?
______ **7.** Do you clean the house every week?

a. Yes, I'm going to Recife, Brazil, for a week.
b. Probably. We love each other.
c. Maybe. She had an interview yesterday.
d. Yes, I do.
e. Yes. An electric one!
f. Usually, but I don't always have time.
g. No, she isn't.

C Use the words to write sentences with *be going to*.

1. she / get a new job / in the city She's going to get a new job in the city.
2. they / get married / next year ______________________________.
3. we / clean the house / on Saturday ______________________________.
4. the Yangs / have a baby ______________________________.
5. my teacher / take a vacation / in August ______________________________.
6. Tanaka / speak English fluently / within two years ______________________________.
7. Mrs. Lopez / buy a new car / in November ______________________________.
8. Gloria and Esteban / buy their own house / in the spring ______________________________.

A 24 Listen and complete the sentences with the correct answer.

1. The speakers are doing a project for ______.
   a. a class b. work c. a website
2. The project is to research a ______ where English is the main language.
   a. country b. environmentalist c. city
3. There are ______ people in the group.
   a. five b. four c. three
4. The group is going to research four ______ the city.
   a. businesses in b. people from c. topics about
5. The group is going to research ______.
   a. Cleveland b. Chicago c. Toronto
6. Kanna is going to research ______.
   a. business b. the environment c. population
7. They are going to do a lot of their research ______.
   a. in class b. online c. with maps
8. The project is going to finish in ______.
   a. one week b. two weeks c. three weeks

B 24 Listen again and complete the chart.

What is the project?	When does the project start and finish?	Who is going to do each part?
	Start: **Finish:**	Kanna: Fernanda: Rodrigo: Luis:

C Put the parts of the project in order.

______ **a.** Group members are going to choose topics.
______ **b.** The group is going to present their research to the class.
______ **c.** They are going to choose a city in an English-speaking country.
______ **d.** Each member is going to do their research.

Lesson C Vocabulary and Grammar

A Complete the sentences with words from the box.

gas	oil	solar	wave	wind	wood

1. Most cars use gasoline or diesel fuel, which both come from ____________.
2. ____________ provides clean, renewable energy, but some people complain that the tall turbines make the landscape ugly.
3. The ocean is the source of powerful ____________ energy.
4. In cold weather, people often build fires with ____________ in their homes.
5. Is the stove electric or ____________?
6. ____________ panels collect sunlight for energy.

B Circle the correct words to complete the sentences.

1. Coal is a form of *renewable* / *non-renewable* energy.
2. *Renewable* / *Non-renewable* energy can always be used.
3. Solar panels are often on top of *buildings* / *wind turbines*.
4. Wood is a natural source of energy, but it is *renewable* / *non-renewable*.
5. Natural gas is often used to *heat homes* / *fuel cars*.
6. *Renewable* / *Non-renewable* energy sources, like coal and oil, won't last.
7. *Coal* / *Wood* comes from deep inside the Earth.

C Rewrite the sentences. Replace *be going to* with *will* or *won't*.

1. People aren't going to stop driving their cars to save energy.
____
2. In the future, there are going to be more electric cars.
____
3. I don't think the US is going to use wave energy.
____
4. In the future, are more countries going to use renewable energy?
____
5. People aren't going to use coal because it makes the air dirty.
____
6. Are scientists going to discover more types of renewable energy?
____
7. My wife and I are going to buy a house with solar panels on the roof.
____
8. There aren't going to be any more non-renewable sources of energy.
____

Children crossing a rope bridge

Building Bridges

In some rural communities around the world, people cannot get to school, a market, or visit the doctor because of a river they cannot cross. Footbridges are a common solution in many places. These basic bridges are often made with rope and pieces of wood. They're not very strong and sometimes fall down.

About 20 years ago, a man in the US saw a photo in a magazine of a person in Ethiopia being hauled over the Blue Nile River on a rope. This was how people crossed the river ever since the old bridge **collapsed**. The image made Ken Frantz, a construction company owner, decide to fix that bridge.

Frantz created a group called Bridges to Prosperity to build the bridge. The group worked with the local people who would use the bridge, and the **tribal elders** gave permission for the project. Donkeys carried supplies to the area, and Frantz, his team, and local volunteers built a lightweight steel bridge in 10 days. Since then, Bridges to Prosperity has built more than 250 bridges in countries around the world.

A safe and reliable footbridge improves the lives of people in rural areas. It means they can bring goods or food to a market to sell. They can possibly earn an income from this. It also means children can go to school and families can visit their relatives on the other side of the river.

collapse fall down
tribal elders older people who make decisions for a tribe

A Read the article. Circle **T** for *true* or **F** for *false*.

1. There are places where not having a bridge is a problem. T F
2. Footbridges are for people to drive across. T F
3. Most footbridges are made of lightweight steel. T F
4. Footbridges can be dangerous. T F
5. A tourist in Ethiopia decided to fix a bridge. T F
6. Ken Frantz saw the problem in a photo in a magazine. T F
7. Frantz had a solution to the problem. T F

B Number the events in the article in order.

_______ **a.** Village elders approved the bridge project.
_______ **b.** The Bridges to Prosperity group was created.
_______ **c.** The group and local volunteers built a new bridge.
_______ **d.** Frantz saw a photo of a dangerous river crossing.
_______ **e.** Bridges to Prosperity built more than 250 bridges.
_______ **f.** Frantz decided to fix the bridge.

C Complete the sentences with *as a result of*, *because*, or *because of*.

1. People cannot go to the market _______________ the river.
2. _______________ the bridge fell down, people crossed the river by rope.
3. Ken Frantz knew about the problem _______________ a photo in a magazine.
4. Bridges to Prosperity was created _______________ Ken's decision to build a bridge.

D Do you think Ken Frantz's reaction to the photo is unusual? Why? Write about another person who solved a problem they learned about from a magazine, the internet, or TV? What was the problem and their solution?

____

____

____

____

____

____

____

A Read about future trends and answer the questions in your notebook. Then fill in the charts.

One population trend is the increase in one-person households. A one-person household is a home where someone lives alone. In the entire world, 15% of households have only one person, and 85% have two or more people. In Japan, the average is higher. There, 32% of households have one person, and 68% have two or more people. In the future, the number of one-person households will probably increase to 38% and the number of households with two or more people will decrease to 62%.

What will increase? What will decrease?

____

One-Person Households in Japan

Present

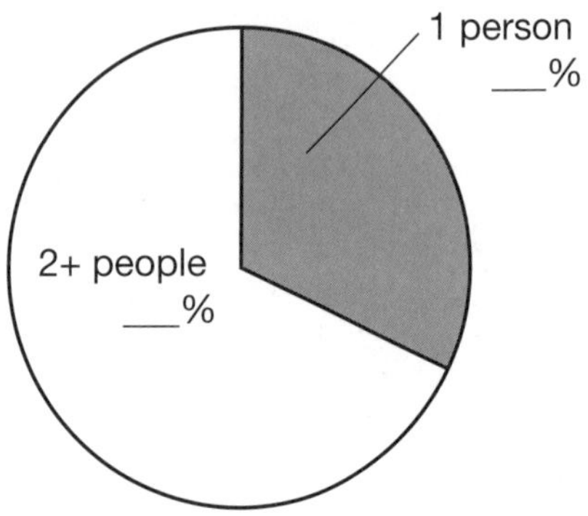

2030

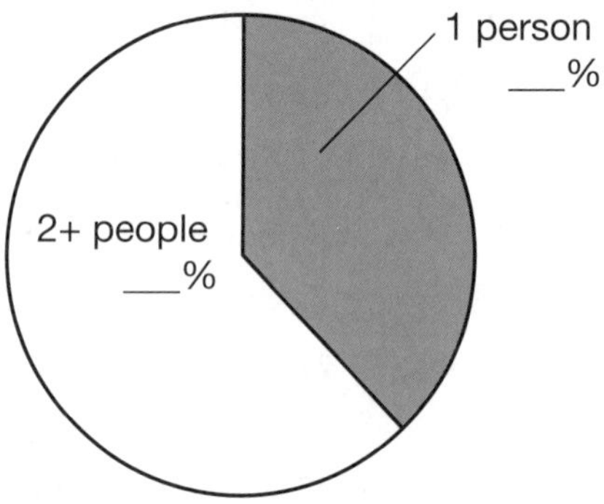

B Look at the charts in **A**. Complete the paragraph with words from the box.

certain	decrease	definitely	increase	probably

It is (1) ____________ that the population is going to increase. The number of people living alone will probably (2) ____________. The number of people living with others will probably (3) ____________. There (4) ____________ won't be enough houses and apartments for more people to live in one-person households. There will (5) ____________ be a need for more houses and apartments.

C Look at the information about how many schools require students to study English and, in your notebook, write a description of the future trends. Use the paragraph in **B** as a model.

Present

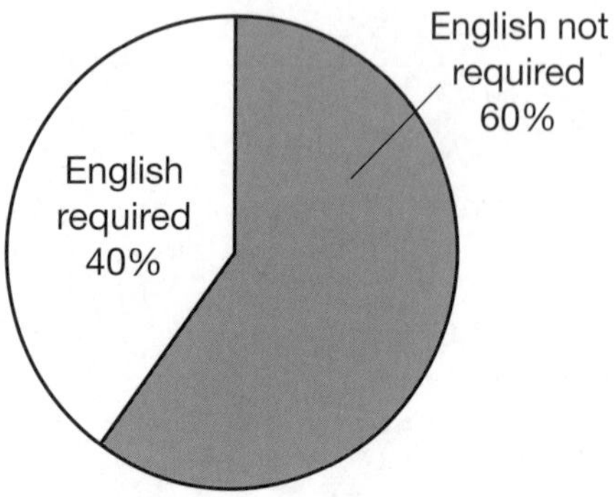

2030

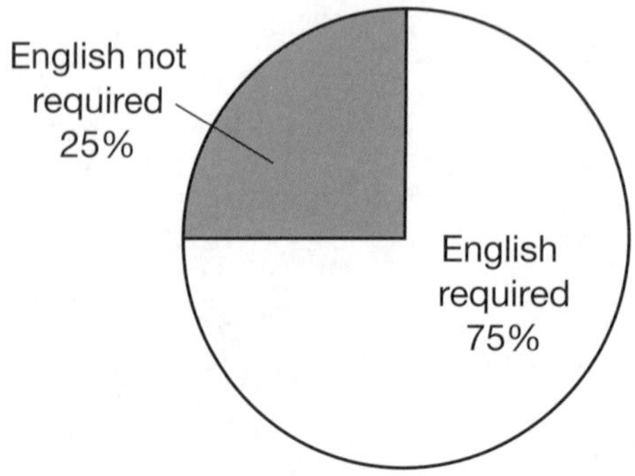

Review

A Complete the questions with *be going to*. Use the pronouns in parentheses.

1. ______________________ speak English fluently? (you)
2. ______________________ buy a new car next year? (she)
3. ______________________ get married in the summer? (they)
4. Who ______________________ do the laundry this week?
5. Where ______________________ go on vacation? (you)
6. When ______________________ buy our own house? (we)
7. ______________________ have children? (you)
8. Who ______________________ pay for dinner?

B Write the questions. Use *be going to* and a question word from the box.

what	when	where	who

1. **A:** ______________________________________? **B:** I'm going to have pizza for dinner.
2. **A:** ______________________________________? **B:** They're going to study in the library.
3. **A:** ______________________________________? **B:** She's going to leave at ten o'clock.
4. **A:** ______________________________________? **B:** Ritika is going to help me.

C Rewrite the *be going to* statements as questions with *will*.

1. People are going to speak more than one language. Will people speak more than one language?
2. The use of wind energy is going to increase. ______________________
3. She is going to study English in Toronto. ______________________
4. He is going to get a new job soon. ______________________
5. Tomas is going to study hard for the next test. ______________________
6. They are going to buy an apartment in the city. ______________________
7. Businesses are going to use more renewable energy. ______________________
8. They're going to put solar panels on their roof. ______________________

D Complete the sentences with *will* or *won't*.

1. In the future, people ____________ burn coal or wood.
2. In the future, more electricity ____________ come from renewable energy sources.
3. ____________ the cost of electricity increase in the future?
4. My country ____________ get electricity from wave energy. We're far from the ocean.
5. ____________ taxis soon be electric cars?
6. In 50 years, ____________ we have robots in our homes?
7. There ____________ be enough drinking water in the future.
8. In about 30 years, most people ____________ live in cities.

Video A Virtual Choir 2,000 Voices Strong

A Read and answer the questions.

1. What is a choir? Have you ever heard a choir sing?

____

2. Do you sing? Do you know anyone who sings well?

____

B Watch the video. Complete the chart.

What is the project?	Who are the people involved?	What are they going to need?

C Write the word or phrase from the box that means the same as the underlined word.

announcement	audition	was in order	filmed scene	participated	thunderstruck

__________ **1.** Eric was <u>amazed</u> when he heard Britilin's voice.
__________ **2.** I sent out this <u>call</u> to singers.
__________ **3.** I had a <u>test performance</u>.
__________ **4.** Many singers <u>joined</u> in the choir.
__________ **5.** They tried until they got just the right <u>take</u>.
__________ **6.** He made sure that everything <u>lined up</u>.

D Answer the question.

As the video shows, a choir is special because many people sing together. What makes this choir different from other choirs? Can you think of another way the internet can bring different people together?

____
____
____
____
____
____
____

Types of Clothing

UNIT 9

Lesson A Vocabulary and Grammar

A Match the sentences.

_______ **1.** I just bought a new pair of pants.	**a.** How much did he spend?
_______ **2.** That's a stylish coat.	**b.** No, they're too tight.
_______ **3.** Do you prefer sneakers or shoes?	**c.** It's a formal party.
_______ **4.** Do you have to wear a suit to work?	**d.** They're very comfortable.
_______ **5.** You should wear a tie.	**e.** No, we can wear casual clothes.
_______ **6.** I'm wearing a hat and gloves.	**f.** Was it expensive?
_______ **7.** He bought an expensive pair of jeans today.	**g.** It's cold outside.
_______ **8.** Are those shoes comfortable?	**h.** Sneakers. They're much more comfortable.

B Circle the correct word.

1. You shouldn't wear that skirt, Monica. It's very *old-fashioned* / *stylish*.

2. My brother's style is very casual. He has one pair of shoes but about 10 pairs of *gloves* / *sneakers*.

3. Edgar packed his suit, shirt, belt, and shoes, but he forgot his *pants* / *tie*.

4. She likes *beautiful* / *cheap* clothes. She always looks very nice.

5. It's polite to take off your *belt* / *hat* when you enter a restaurant.

6. These pants don't fit. They're very *expensive* / *tight*.

7. I need a new *heavy* / *light* coat for the winter.

C Complete the sentences. Use the comparative form of the adjective in parentheses.

1. The long skirt is ________________ (formal) than the short one.

2. The purple tie is ugly, and the orange tie is even ________________ (ugly).

3. Sometimes new jeans are tight and ________________ (comfortable) than old jeans.

4. These shoes were ________________ (expensive) than my sneakers, but they're less comfortable!

5. The nylon shirt is ________________ (cheap) than the silk one.

6. Buying shoes in a store is ________________ (good) than shopping online.

7. The purple blouse is ________________ (nice) than the white one.

D Unscramble the words to make sentences.

1. more formal / jeans and a t-shirt / than / is / a suit ________________________________.

2. comfortable / are / loose ones / tight clothes / than / less ________________________.

3. look / better / a belt / pants / with ________________________________.

4. you / wear / a lighter / because / jacket / should / it's warm out ____________________.

5. Sofia / than / more / her / is / sister / stylish ________________________________.

6. Miguel's ripped jeans / than / are / Jose's black jeans / trendier ____________________.

A 26 Listen to the conversation. Read the sentences. Then circle **T** for *true* or **F** for *false*.

▲ A woman wearing a scarf.

1. The woman wants to buy a scarf for the winter. T F
2. The scarf is a gift for a friend. T F
3. Her friend likes colors like black and brown. T F
4. The silk scarfs are the most expensive. T F
5. The cheapest silk scarf is $75. T F
6. The silk scarfs are smaller than the cotton ones. T F
7. The woman buys an orange scarf made of cotton. T F
8. The woman pays for the scarf with her card. T F

B 26 Listen again and put the parts of the conversation in order.

_______ **a.** The woman pays $29 for a cotton scarf.
_______ **b.** The cheapest silk scarf is more expensive than the cotton scarfs.
_______ **c.** The salesman shows her some wool scarfs.
_______ **d.** The silk scarf is very soft, and very expensive.
_______ **e.** The woman is shopping for a gift for her friend.
_______ **f.** She wants a stylish scarf her friend can wear with a blouse or sweater.

C Who asks the questions and says the sentences below? Write *S* (salesperson) or *C* (customer).

_______ **1.** Hello, can I help you?
_______ **2.** It's a gift for her birthday.
_______ **3.** They're made of wool.
_______ **4.** There are some very nice silk ones over here.
_______ **5.** How about this?
_______ **6.** And it's very soft.
_______ **7.** Do you have anything cheaper?
_______ **8.** They're bigger than the silk scarfs and less expensive!
_______ **9.** And cotton is easier to clean.
_______ **10.** How much is this green one?
_______ **11.** OK, I'll take it.
_______ **12.** Are you paying with cash or card?

Lesson C Vocabulary and Grammar

A Look at the pictures. Write questions and answers. Use words from the box.

cotton	leather	silk	synthetic materials	wool

1.
a. What are the gloves made of?
b. They're made of leather.

2.
a. ______
b. ______

3.
a. ______
b. ______

4.
a. ______
b. ______

5.
a. ______
b. ______

6.
a. ______
b. ______

B Complete the sentences. Use the superlative form of the adjective in parentheses.

1. Leather is ______ (good) material for shoes and boots.
2. ______ (cheap) pants are made of polyester.
3. The hats made of wool are ______ (warm).
4. The silk socks are ______ (expensive) ones.
5. Linen and silk are two of ______ (light) materials for clothes.
6. In my opinion, clothes made of cotton are ______ (comfortable).

C Find the error with the superlative in each sentence. Change the sentence so it is correct.

1. The good silk is made in Thailand.
2. What is the lighter natural material?
3. The cotton jacket is the less expensive, but it's not the warmest.
4. The most pretty dress is also the most expensive one.
5. Those are the uglier sneakers in the whole store.
6. You should wear your most heavy sweater and jacket to go skiing.

Fast Fashion

[1] The phrase *fast fashion* describes the trendiest clothes available at the lowest prices. The prices are low because the stores want their customers to return very soon—maybe even the next week—to buy more of the newest fashions. Some of these fast fashion stores display new clothes weekly or even twice a week!

[2] In the traditional fashion industry, new styles come out four times a year. This schedule follows the four seasons: spring, summer, fall, and winter. In the fast fashion industry, a new "season" happens every month or so. Fast fashion makes a lot of money because there are more selling seasons within one year.

[3] One important reason why fast fashion is less expensive than traditional fashion is that the quality is worse. A trendy shirt from a fast fashion store doesn't need to last for years because it won't be stylish next season. Trendy clothes usually won't last because the materials used to make them are cheap and not as good quality. For example, in a fast fashion store, you are more likely to find a sweater made of acrylic, a synthetic material, than wool.

[4] Some people think fast fashion is good because it means they can buy stylish clothes at low prices. Others disagree. They think that fast fashion creates a lot of waste. Since the early 2000s, when the fast fashion trend started, the production of clothes has doubled. Now people are buying more clothes, and are wearing them for shorter amounts of time. This means clothes are thrown out because clothes that aren't good quality can't be given to someone else.

[5] Finally, clothing manufacturing can be bad for the environment. Producing many materials, even natural ones such as cotton, requires huge amounts of water. Making synthetic materials can involve oil and other chemicals which can cause pollution. And dyes used to color clothes are also a source of pollution.

[6] Before buying the latest fashions, customers should read about their favorite clothing brands online. There is information available about which clothing makers are more responsible than others.

▼ Fast fashion has new seasons as often as once a month.

A Look at the photo. Answer the questions.

1. Is this clothing store for men or women? ______
2. Does this look like a store that sells the latest fashion trends? Why?
______
3. Do you think the clothes in this store are expensive? Why? ______
______
4. Have you heard the phrase *fast fashion*? What do you think it means?
______

B Read the article. Circle **T** for *true* or **F** for *false*.

1. Fast fashion is stylish and inexpensive.	T	F
2. You can find new clothes at fast fashion stores every month or so.	T	F
3. Fast fashion and the traditional fashion industry have the same seasons.	T	F
4. Usually fast fashion clothes aren't the best quality.	T	F
5. Fast fashion goes out of style quickly.	T	F
6. Some people like fast fashion because of the high-quality clothes at low prices.	T	F
7. Some people don't like fast fashion because it's traditional and old-fashioned.	T	F
8. As a result of fast fashion, more clothes are being produced.	T	F

C What do the sentences describe? Write *F* (fast fashion) or *T* (traditional fashion).

______ **1.** Trendy clothes that are stylish right now.
______ **2.** There are new clothes in the store every spring, summer, winter, and fall.
______ **3.** The clothes are made from the best materials.
______ **4.** The clothes aren't made to last a long time.
______ **5.** The prices usually aren't low.
______ **6.** People can buy more of this fashion because the clothes are cheap.
______ **7.** This kind of fashion became popular about 20 years ago.

D Match the paragraph number (1–6) with the main idea.

______ **a.** The good and bad points of fast fashion
______ **b.** Fashion seasons
______ **c.** How customers can learn about brands
______ **d.** An explanation of fast fashion
______ **e.** Clothing manufacturing and the environment
______ **f.** The quality and materials of fast fashion

A Read the sentences from advertisements and put the adjectives in the correct order.

1. For sale! A pair of (red / soft / leather) ________________ gloves. Made in Argentina, bought a year ago.
2. Like new! Designer sneakers, men's size 11. They're (stylish / black / comfortable) ________________ and, in my opinion, go with casual or fomal clothes.
3. Only worn once! A (blue / large / comfortable) ________________ raincoat. It's made of a synthetic material. The lining is soft cotton.
4. My son wore this (wool / warm / green) ________________ winter coat only once because it was tight on him. Child's size 4.
5. (black / expensive / leather / Italian) ________________ handbag made by famous designer. Great gift idea!

B Read the ad. Answer the questions.

1. What is the seller's opinion of the sweater? ________________
2. Is it new? ________________
3. What color is it? ________________
4. What is it made of? ________________
5. What size is it? ________________
6. How does it fit? ________________

Beautiful, new, gray, Irish, wool women's sweater. This good-quality, soft wool is lightweight. It keeps you warm, but it's not heavy. Buttons on the front. Size 8–10. The fit is loose and comfortable, not tight.
Price $40

C What type of clothing is your country known for? Is there a traditional way of dressing or a famous brand from there? Think of an item of clothing from your country and write an ad for it. Use the order of adjectives in the box to help you.

your opinion	size	age	color	nationality	material	other details

____

____

____

____

____

____

____

____

Review

UNIT 9

A Complete the sentences. Use the comparative form of the adjective in parentheses.

1. I like trendy clothes, but my roommate wears ________________ (traditional) clothes.
2. Sneakers are usually ________________ (expensive) than nice leather shoes.
3. The heavy wool sweater feels ________________ (rough) than the light one.
4. Ties made of synthetic material are ________________ (cheap) than silk ones.
5. The cotton shirt is ________________ (good) quality than the polyester one.
6. He needed to look ________________ (formal), so he wore a suit to the interview.
7. The red hat is ________________ (pretty) than the black one.
8. In my opinion, the brown shoes are ________________ (bad) than the blue ones.

B Write sentences with comparative adjectives.

1. (this wool sweater / warm / that raincoat) This wool sweater is warmer than that raincoat.
2. (sneakers / comfortable / shoes) ________________.
3. (jeans and a shirt / formal / a suit) ________________.
4. (this wool hat / good / that baseball cap) ________________.
5. (a shirt / light / a sweater) ________________.
6. (this blouse / nice / that blouse) ________________.
7. (the black coat / cheap / the white coat) ________________.
8. (leather shoes / expensive / plastic shoes) ________________.

C Unscramble the questions in the conversation.

Salesperson: (you / can / help / I) (1) ________________?

Customer: Yes. I'd like a sweater to go with these pants.

Salesperson: (what / are / you / size) (2) ________________?

Customer: I'm a 12.

Salesperson: (this / what / about / sweater) (3) ________________?

Customer: It's very nice. (is / it / much / how) (4) ________________?

Salesperson: It's $120.

Customer: Hmmm . . . (anything / do / you / expensive / have / less) (5) ________________?

Salesperson: This one's on sale for $45.

Customer: (can / on / I / it / try) (6) ________________?

Salesperson: Yes, the dressing rooms are over there.

Video How Your T-shirt Can Make a Difference

A Read the facts about water use. Do they surprise you? Why? Choose one fact and write a sentence explaining your reason.

1. Water is the most common substance found on Earth.
2. One cycle of an automatic dishwasher uses 12 to 20 gallons of water.
3. It takes about 120 gallons of water to produce one egg.
4. Producing a Sunday newspaper requires about 150 gallons of water.
5. Producing a typical fast-food meal (hamburger, French fries, and a soda) requires about 1,400 gallons of water.
6. Production of the cotton for a pair of jeans uses about 1,800 gallons of water.
7. Water makes up almost two-thirds of the human body, and 70 percent of the brain.

____

____

B Watch the video and read the sentences. Then circle **T** for *true* or **F** for *false*.

1.	Cottonseed oil is a food some people use.	T	F
2.	Dollar bills are made from paper only.	T	F
3.	Cotton has a big impact on the planet.	T	F
4.	It takes 270 liters of water to make one t-shirt.	T	F
5.	Producing t-shirts uses enough water for a person to drink for more than 2 years.	T	F
6.	One load of washing uses 5X more energy than drying.	T	F
7.	Drying clothes in a dryer doesn't use a lot of energy.	T	F

C Write the correct percentages to complete the sentences.

Water is the most common substance found on Earth. But (1) ______________% of the water is salty. Another (2) ______________ % is frozen in the form of snow and ice. So, about (3) ______________% of the Earth's water is available for use. And (4) ______________% of that 1% goes to growing crops.

D Answer the questions.

1. How many loads of laundry do you or your family do every week? ______________________________

   ____

2. If you have a dryer, do you dry every load of laundry? Why? ______________________________

   ____

3. After watching the video, do you think you will use water more carefully? If yes, how will you do that?

   ____

   ____

   ____

Lifestyles

UNIT **10**

Lesson A Vocabulary and Grammar

A Match the words and meanings.

_______ **1.** lifestyle
_______ **2.** be in bad shape
_______ **3.** work out
_______ **4.** be in good shape
_______ **5.** junk food
_______ **6.** sunbathing
_______ **7.** eat a balanced diet

a. have an unhealthy body
b. exercise in a gym
c. eat different kinds of healthy food
d. have a healthy body
e. sitting or lying in the sun
f. how you live
g. unhealthy food like candy, chips, and cookies

B Complete the sentences with the words from **A**.

Anton and Petrul are brothers. Anton has a good job, but he doesn't have a healthy (1) ________________. He works long hours in front of a computer. He doesn't take breaks, or (2) ________________ regularly. He belongs to a gym, but he never (3) ________________ there. He says he doesn't have time. As a result, he (4) ________________.

On the other hand, Petrul has a (5) ________________ lifestyle. Petrul also works hard, but he (6) ________________. He rides his bike to work. He belongs to the same gym as his brother, but unlike Anton, he (7) ________________ three times a week. Petrul tries not to eat (8) ________________. He's learning to cook healthy food. He cooks for Anton sometimes, because he wants Anton to eat (9) ________________ meals, too.

C How strong is the advice in each sentence? Circle the correct answer.

1. You should go to bed earlier.	gentle	strong	very strong
2. You have to quit smoking.	gentle	strong	very strong
3. You could eat salad for lunch.	gentle	strong	very strong
4. You could go to the gym after work.	gentle	strong	very strong
5. You must stop eating so much sugar.	gentle	strong	very strong
6. You shouldn't drink so much coffee.	gentle	strong	very strong
7. You could go to bed an hour earlier.	gentle	strong	very strong
8. You have to change your lifestyle.	gentle	strong	very strong

Lesson B Listening

A 28 Listen. Circle **T** for *true* or **F** for *false*.

1. Hiroto travels for work. T F
2. Ivan cooks and eats fresh food. T F
3. Gloria drinks a lot of energy drinks. T F
4. Gloria gets a lot of sleep. T F
5. Ivan gets exercise as a part of his job. T F
6. Hiroto doesn't like to cook. T F
7. Hiroto gets the most exercise. T F
8. Gloria thinks that drinking coffee is a bad habit. T F
9. Ivan doesn't like seafood. T F
10. Hiroto often eats protein bars. T F

B 28 Listen again. Check (✓) the correct name(s).

	Hiroto	Ivan	Gloria
1. Who exercises?			
2. Who has a stressful job?			
3. Who eats unhealthy food?			
4. Who doesn't have time to exercise?			
5. Who drinks a lot of coffee?			
6. Who doesn't get enough sleep?			
7. Who exercises as part of their job?			
8. Who spends their time off with family?			

C 28 Listen again. Write an unhealthy habit of each person. Then, write a sentence giving advice to that person using a modal (*could*, *should*, *must*, or *have to*).

1. **Hiroto**
   - **a.** Unhealthy habit: eats protein bars and drinks energy drinks
   - **b.** Advice: ______________________________
2. **Ivan**
   - **a.** Unhealthy habit: ______________________________
   - **b.** Advice: ______________________________
3. **Gloria**
   - **a.** Unhealthy habit: ______________________________
   - **b.** Advice: ______________________________

Lesson C Vocabulary and Grammar

A Complete the compound adjectives.

1. (delicious) mouth ____________________
2. (not from a factory) home ____________________
3. (makes you happy) heart ____________________
4. (for your whole life) life ____________________
5. (relaxing) stress- ____________________
6. (too busy) over ____________________
7. (without a lot of calories) low- ____________________
8. (from your own garden) home ____________________

B Complete the sentences with the compound adjectives in **A**.

1. Stephen started writing stories when he was eight. His ____________ dream is to be an author.
2. Mrs. Ting can sew very well. As a result, her daughters often wear ____________ dresses.
3. She often falls asleep on the bus on the way home from work. She must be ____________.
4. Hinata needs to lose weight, so she is eating ____________ food for the next month.
5. Mr. Garcia wants a ____________ job.
6. Maria made a delicious sauce with ____________ tomatoes from her garden.
7. More than a million people liked the ____________ video on social media.
8. Emilio's Restaurant is famous for it's ____________ pizza.

C A reporter is interviewing Anton Muskov, a famous basketball player. Write questions with *how*.

Reporter: How (1) ________________________________ play basketball?

Anton: I play five times a week. That's every day from Monday to Friday.

Reporter: (2) ________________________________?

Anton: I take a break twice a week. On the weekend I like to relax at home.

Reporter: (3) ________________________________?

Anton: Oh, I get about nine hours of sleep a night. I go to bed early and wake up early to practice.

Reporter: (4) ________________________________?

Anton: I'm 23 years old.

Reporter: (5) ________________________________?

Anton: There are five people in my family—my mother, my father, my two sisters, and me.

Healthy Habits

Everyone wants to live a long and healthy life. Researchers studying longevity, or how long a person lives, look at people's lifestyles, including their habits. They do this because they want to know which habits help people live longer.

In 1970, some scientists asked 7,000 people in the United States about their habits. Then, they checked to see how long the people lived. The scientists learned that the people with the longest lives:

1. ate breakfast every day.
2. didn't eat snacks between meals.
3. weren't too heavy or too thin.
4. exercised regularly.
5. slept seven to eight hours every night—no more, no less.
6. didn't smoke.
7. drank plenty of water every day.

These seven habits made a big difference. People who did all of these things lived 12 years longer than people who did only one, two, or three.

Habits are unlike other longevity **factors**—such as **genes** or environment—because people can change their habits. It's not always easy, but it's possible to learn good habits and break bad ones.

So, how can people change their habits? Scientists say to make changes slowly. It's important to have clear goals. A goal like "live a healthier lifestyle" sounds good, but isn't clear. How will you do this exactly? A clearer goal is, for example, to take a walk every evening, or to stop eating snacks between meals. And to break a bad habit, some experts suggest replacing it. For example, if a person is trying to quit smoking, they should drink a glass of water or go for a short walk when they feel like they want a cigarette. Experts also say you should be patient. Changing habits takes time, and nobody does it perfectly the first time.

factor one thing that influences a situation
genes cells in your body with information passed down from your parents that decides how you will develop (for example, to have blue eyes or to be tall)

The study says that healthy habits like regular exercise can help people live longer lives.

A Read the article. What does it say about each habit? Circle *good*, *bad*, or *no information*.

1. Eating eggs and fruit for breakfast every day	good	bad	no information
2. Not getting enough sleep	good	bad	no information
3. Going to the doctor often	good	bad	no information
4. Going for a walk every night	good	bad	no information
5. Being too thin	good	bad	no information
6. Drinking plenty of water every day	good	bad	no information
7. Exercising every day	good	bad	no information
8. Smoking	good	bad	no information

B Circle the correct word to complete each sentence.

1. A study of longevity looks at how *long* / *well* a person lives.

2. The scientists in the article wanted information about people's *diets* / *habits*.

3. Drinking coffee every day *is* / *isn't* one of the seven healthy habits.

4. Not getting enough sleep is a(n) *healthy* / *unhealthy* habit.

5. When you stop a bad habit, you *break it* / *pick it up*.

6. An example of a *clear* / *unclear* goal is to eat at least five vegetables a day.

7. Experts say people *could* / *should* make changes slowly.

C Read the advice about changing habits. Check (✓) the sentences that agree with the article.

- ☐ **1.** People should make changes slowly.
- ☐ **2.** It's not necessary to have goals.
- ☐ **3.** People should replace a bad habit with something.
- ☐ **4.** It doesn't take much time to learn good habits.
- ☐ **5.** It's important to have clear goals.
- ☐ **6.** People have to understand that it takes time to change their habits.
- ☐ **7.** Drinking a glass of water with every meal is a clear goal.

D Answer the questions.

1. How many of the seven habits do you have? Which ones? ______________________________

____

____

2. Which of the habits do you think is the easiest to keep? Why? __________________________

____

____

3. Which of the habits do you think is the hardest to keep? Why? __________________________

____

____

A Read the paragraph. Write the numbers of the sentences in the paragraph.

[1] I love hiking. [2] I go almost every weekend with a group. [3] First, I love being in nature, and hiking through forests and up and down hills is my favorite thing to do. [4] Of course, the exercise and fresh air are good for my health, too. [5] In addition, it's a social activity because the other hikers and I talk as we walk. [6] I've made some great friends this way. [7] Finally, when I use maps and plan routes I have to exercise my brain as well as my body. [8] To sum up, I think hiking is something all people should do to get healthy and enjoy nature.

_______ **a.** Topic sentence _______ **b.** Supporting sentences _______ **c.** Concluding sentence

B Read the paragraph. Underline the sentences that give advice.

[1] In my opinion, my friend Gustavo's video game playing is out of control. [2] He has to stop playing during the week. [3] He should delete all of the games from his cell phone, too. [4] Then he won't always play video games on the bus, between classes, and in the library. [5] He should only play them on the weekend. [6] Maybe he could make a goal to put away his gaming devices two hours before he goes to bed. [7] In conclusion, he must do something to break his bad gaming habit.

C Write the numbers of the sentences in the paragraph in **B**.

_______ **a.** Topic sentence _______ **b.** Supporting sentences _______ **c.** Concluding sentence

D Write a paragraph giving advice to someone about starting a good habit or breaking a bad habit.

____

____

____

____

____

____

____

____

____

Review

A Complete the conversations with words from the box.

bad	exercise	healthy	junk food	lifestyle	shape	sleep	work out

1. **A:** I'm in ________________ shape.
   B: You could ________________ at the gym after class.
2. **A:** Does he eat a lot of ________________?
   B: No, he has a very ________________ diet.
3. **A:** Is drinking a lot of water part of a healthy ________________?
   B: Yes, of course! And you should drink water after you ________________.
4. **A:** Mario and Yuna are in very good ________________.
   B: Yes, they are. They ride their bikes to work every day.
5. **A:** Andrei stays up late watching TV most nights.
   B: He should get more ________________.

B Complete the sentences with modals.

1. **Doctor to patient:** You ____have to____ stop smoking right now!
2. **Friend to friend:** You ________________ drink water instead of soda.
3. **Mother to son:** You ________________ eat all of your vegetables if you want dessert!
4. **Teacher to student:** You ________________ study the new vocabulary. It's on the test!
5. **Friend to friend:** You ________________ try to lose weight.
6. **Parent to child:** You ________________ wear a helmet when you ride your bike.
7. **Grandchild to grandparent:** You ________________ turn off your phone when you don't want to answer it.
8. **Personal trainer to client:** You ________________ listen to music when you exercise.

C Circle the best word to complete each sentence.

1. The movie tells the *heartwarming* / *lifelong* story of a child's love for his pet dog.
2. Yasmin and Felipe go hiking *about* / *almost* twice a month.
3. *Homegrown* / *Homemade* bread tastes better than bread from the store.
4. They go to the movies *not much* / *around* once a month.
5. *Overworked* / *Stress-free* employees are usually unhappy with their jobs.
6. Miguel is my *homegrown* / *lifelong* friend.

Video Living Past 100

A This video is about a region in China where many people live to be 100 or more. Tourists visit because they want to learn about the lifestyle. Does this sound like a place you would like to visit? Why?

____

____

____

B Watch the video. Complete the sentences with numbers from the video.

1. A centenarian is a person who is ______ years old or older.
2. In Bama County, the number of people over the age of ______ is nearly ______ times the number the rest of China.
3. For more than ______ years, villager Huang Zhongkang has gone fishing every day.
4. Huang Zhongkang is ______ years old.
5. One man believes he is the oldest person in the village. He is ______ years old. His son, aged ______, explains why he has lived so long.
6. One health tourist, Yao Xuchu, had a stroke ______ years ago.

C Circle the person who said each statement.

1. "It's the environment here that makes people generally live longer."
   a. researcher **b.** villager **c.** health tourist
2. "For more than 30 years, I have gone fishing every day. This lifestyle is carefree."
   a. researcher **b.** villager **c.** health tourist
3. "I'd rather live in the village than in the urban area."
   a. researcher **b.** villager **c.** health tourist
4. "The secret to our longevity is very simple. We eat what we plant."
   a. researcher **b.** villager **c.** health tourist
5. "Every day, I come here to sing very beautiful songs."
   a. researcher **b.** villager **c.** health tourist
6. "As long as tourists don't litter here, we welcome the development."
   a. researcher **b.** villager **c.** health tourist

D Health tourism will bring income to the villages, but tourism can cause litter and pollution. How do you think tourism will change Bama County? Will the change be good or bad? ______________________________

____

____

____

____

____

____

____

Achievements

UNIT 11

Lesson A Vocabulary and Grammar

A Complete each sentence with a verb from the box.

buys	cleans	cooks	don't clean	takes out	vacuums	walks	wash

1. Luis ________________ the groceries on Saturday morning.
2. My sisters ________________ their rooms every week.
3. Neftali ________________ his dog twice a day.
4. Alonso never ________________ the trash.
5. Every weekend, Sorin ________________ his car.
6. Fumiko always ________________ the floor before she washes it.
7. Veronica and her father ________________ the dishes together.
8. Mrs. Tanaka usually ________________ dinner for her family.

B Unscramble the present perfect sentences.

1. his / Jose / room / cleaned / has ________________________________
2. the / has / she / groceries / bought ________________________________?
3. out / I / no, / haven't / trash / taken / the ________________________________
4. cleaned / Monica and Jaime / their / have / car ________________________________
5. dishes / have / the / they / washed ________________________________?
6. the / you / have / living room / floor / vacuumed ________________________________?

C Complete the present perfect questions and answers. Use the verbs in parentheses.

1. **A:** ________________ you ________________ (study) for the test?
   B: Yes, ________________.
2. **A:** What ________________ she ________________ (cook) for dinner?
   B: She ________________ fish.
3. **A:** ________________ Dad ________________ (buy) the groceries yet?
   B: No, he ________________. He's at the store now.
4. **A:** ________________ they ________________ (arrive) yet?
   B: No, ________________.

D Find and correct the mistake in each sentence or question.

1. Have he washed the dishes?
2. They has cleaned the car.
3. What have you learn?
4. No, I hasn't read that book.

Lesson B Listening

A Read the job ad. Answer the questions.

> **NOW HIRING!**
>
> Technology Store Assistant
>
> —A busy technology store needs a sales assistant to help with customers.
>
> —We are looking for a helpful person with good communication skills in both English and Spanish.
>
> —Sales experience is not necessary (training is provided).
>
> —An interest in technology and devices (laptops, tablets, and smartphones) is an advantage.

1. What is the job? ______________________

2. What skills do you need for the job?

____

____

____

____

B 30 Read the ad again. Write five questions for the job interview. Then listen and check (✓) any of your questions that you hear in the interview.

1. ______________________

2. ______________________

3. ______________________

4. ______________________

5. ______________________

C 30 Listen again. Answer the questions.

1. Why does Mr. Vargas want the job? ______________________

____

2. Is Mr. Vargas a helpful person? What example does he give? ______________________

____

3. What languages does he speak? ______________________

4. Has he worked in a store? ______________________

5. What work experience does he have? ______________________

____

6. Is Mr. Vargas a good person for the job? ______________________

Lesson C Vocabulary and Grammar

A Circle the correct word to complete each sentence.

1. It takes a long time to *learn* / *pass* a language.
2. Laura and Beatriz are going to *get* / *travel* abroad this summer.
3. Antonio wants to *pass* / *run* the Chicago Marathon.
4. My son *graduated* / *passed* from high school in June.
5. Cesar *got* / *took* a promotion at work.
6. Mrs. Sanchez *passed* / *graduated* her driving test on Saturday.

B Match the sentence halves.

_______ **1.** He has gotten
_______ **2.** Have you graduated
_______ **3.** Eva has learned
_______ **4.** No, I haven't passed
_______ **5.** Marcos has run
_______ **6.** Has he ever traveled

a. two marathons!
b. the driving test.
c. abroad?
d. two promotions in the last year.
e. from college?
f. a new language.

C Underline the present perfect verb forms and circle the simple past verb forms.

A: Have you had a job interview yet?
B: No, I haven't, but I've emailed my resume to a lot of companies.
A: Which companies did you send it to?
B: Mostly large, international ones. I've worked in Europe and it has been my dream to return there.
A: When did you work there?
B: About two years ago. I worked in Germany before I graduated from college.
A: Wow! I've never worked abroad, but I studied in Scotland for a year.
B: How was that?
A: It was great. And my English improved a lot.

D Complete the conversations with the simple past and the present perfect.

1. **A:** _______________ you ever _______________ (get) a promotion?
   B: Yes, I have. Two years ago, I _______________ (be) promoted to manager.
2. **A:** _______________ Kanna ever _______________ (run) a marathon?
   B: No, she _______________. But she _______________ (run) two half-marathons.
3. **A:** _______________ your kids _______________ (graduate) from college?
   B: Yes, they both _______________ (graduate) within the last two years.
4. **A:** _______________ you _______________ (study) abroad?
   B: Yes, I have. I _______________ (study) in London for one year.

Professor Stephen Hawking

Amazing Achievements: Stephen Hawking

Stephen Hawking was one of the most famous scientists of this century. As a cosmologist and a theoretical physicist, he used mathematics to study space and the universe. He wrote several popular science books. He wrote *A Brief History of Time* in 1988, and more than 10 million people have bought this book. In his lifetime, many other scientists said Hawking was the greatest scientist in the world.

Hawking faced difficult problems in his life. When he was 21, he got a serious disease called ALS. The disease quickly got worse, and soon he couldn't walk or speak. He could only move his left hand. He used a wheelchair with a motor to get around. He "talked" by typing words into a computer. Then, the computer pronounced the words for him.

But, for Hawking, his work was more important than his problems. He was interested in the beginning of the universe. He taught at Cambridge University in England and gave lectures at other universities. He wrote many important scientific papers and won many prizes for his work. He appeared in several movies and was on TV many times. He traveled in countries around the world, and in 2007, he went up on a special zero gravity plane.

Hawking's achievements are truly amazing. Even though his body was in a wheelchair, his mind explored the universe. Hawking died in March, 2018. He was 76.

A Complete the sentences.

_______	**1.** Hawking was a	**a.** when he got a serious disease.
_______	**2.** He studied	**b.** using a computer.
_______	**3.** *A Brief History of Time*	**c.** the universe.
_______	**4.** Hawking was a young man	**d.** Cambridge University.
_______	**5.** He was able to "speak"	**e.** scientist.
_______	**6.** He taught at	**f.** is a popular book by Hawking.

B Read the sentences. Then circle **T** for *true* or **F** for *false*.

1. Hawking used mathematics to study space.	T	F
2. He wrote a book called *The History of Everything* in 1988.	T	F
3. Other scientists thought his achievements were great.	T	F
4. Hawking was in a wheelchair as a result of an accident.	T	F
5. He was unable to speak without using a computer.	T	F
6. He wasn't in a movie.	T	F

C Complete the sentences about Hawking's achievements.

1. He wrote ____.

2. Other scientists called him ________________________________.

3. He ______________________ scientific papers.

4. He won ______________________.

5. He ______________________ in movies.

6. He was on ______________________ many times.

7. He ______________________ around the world.

8. In 2007, he went up on a ______________________.

D Match each word from the article to the meaning.

_______	**1.** century	**a.** investigate
_______	**2.** several	**b.** relating to science
_______	**3.** scientific	**c.** 100 years
_______	**4.** explore	**d.** a few

A 32 Listen. Complete the sentences.

1. In my country, resumes don't include ________________ information like birth date.
2. You should include a few important ________________ about your work experience.
3. Make sure your email ________________ is correct on your resume.
4. Do you have any work ________________?
5. Cesar has a ________________ degree from New York University.
6. Have you worked with ________________?
7. She got her driver's ________________ in December.
8. What are your other ________________?

B Circle five spelling mistakes and five mistakes with capital letters in this description.

Hello. My name is Silvia Marquez. I'm from Guadalajara, mexico. I graduted from the University of guadalajara last Year. I studied busines and english. I have Work Experence in the financial aid office of the unversity. I have excellent computer skils. My Interests are horses and cooking.

C Circle and correct the five spelling mistakes and five mistakes with capital letters in this resume.

Juliana Sousa

4387 Cypress avenue, Apt. 17
Coral Gables, Florida 33124

email: juli-sousa18@sousa.br
phone: +1 (989) 555-8237

Education

2018–Present	MA, Busieness Administration and management, University of Miami
2014–2017	BA, English and Finance

Work Experience

June 2017–Jun 2018	Junior Financial Analyst, GreenSource investments

Skills

Languages: Portuguese, English, Spanish
computers: Word, Excel, PowerPoint
Florida driver's licenze

Interests

Member of Saving the Waves, a local environmental Group. Volunteer at the Childern's Hopsital.

Reference

Dr. Eleanor Matsuzuki, Professor of Business Studies, University of Miami

Review

A Complete the sentences with the verbs in parentheses. Use the present perfect.

1. Mr. Feria ________________ (interview) three people for the job.
2. Enrique ________________ (prepare) his resume very carefully.
3. The students ________________ (never, travel) abroad.
4. ________________ you ________________ (visit) your grandparents recently?
5. The woman ________________ (speak) in front of a big group many times.
6. Finally, Larissa ________________ (pass) the driving test.
7. ________________ she ________________ (manage) people before?
8. ________________ they ________________ (hire) a person for the job?

B Write statements and questions using the words below and the present perfect.

1. you / ever / be / to Korea ________________________________
2. what / you / cook / for dinner ________________________________
3. Manuela / vacuum and wash / the floors ________________________________
4. Tomas and Paulo / finish / studying for the test ________________________________
5. Sofia / travel / to China / twice for her job ________________________________
6. where / you / be ________________________________

C Circle the correct form of the verb.

1. Laura *traveled* / *has traveled* to Europe three times. Last year, she *went* / *has gone* to Spain.
2. Our class *finished* / *has finished* 10 units of *World English* so far.
3. Anita *passed* / *has passed* her driving test last week.
4. Ren is a TV reporter. He *met* / *has met* many famous people.
5. I *know* / *have known* my best friend all my life.
6. Souta *started* / *has started* a new job in October.
7. I *ran* / *have run* a marathon in 2018.

D Have you done these things? In your notebook, write sentences with the present perfect and simple past.

1. eat Korean food (what?)
   a. *I've eaten Korean food.* or *I've never eaten Korean food.*
   b. *I ate a noodle dish called japchae.*
2. graduate from high school (when?)
3. travel abroad (where?)
4. watch a movie in English (which one?)

Video Wasfia's Journey

A Read the facts about Wasfia Nazreen's country, Bangladesh. Then watch the video and answer the question.

1. Bangladesh became a country in 1971.
2. The capital is Dhaka.
3. The population is about 160 million people.
4. Bangladesh is the most densely populated country in the world.
5. Almost half of the population is under 25 years of age.

Wasfia says her climb is for the youth of her country. Which fact above do you think is most important to her?

____

B Read the sentences. Then circle **T** for *true* or **F** for *false*.

1. Most people Wasfia meets know something about her country.	T	F
2. Wasfia explains that life is not easy for women in Bagladesh.	T	F
3. People didn't believe Wasfia could climb all seven mountains.	T	F
4. Wasfia didn't do enough training.	T	F
5. Someone very important to Wasfia died in an accident.	T	F
6. The two girls in the video are Wasfia's daughters.	T	F
7. Wasfia says more girls should be mountain climbers when they grow up.	T	F
8. Wasfia was the first Bangladeshi to climb all seven summits.	T	F

C Match each word from the video to the meaning.

______	**1.** highlight	**a.** things that stop you
______	**2.** obstacles	**b.** stop fighting
______	**3.** constantly	**c.** necessary
______	**4.** essential	**d.** to win
______	**5.** campaign	**e.** to follow something
______	**6.** pursue	**f.** give special attention to
______	**7.** surrender	**g.** non-stop
______	**8.** conquer	**h.** a plan to reach a goal

D Answer the question.

Describe a goal that you have achieved. What did you do to reach that goal?

____

____

____

____

____

____

Decisions

UNIT 12

Lesson A Vocabulary and Grammar

A Complete the sentences with the words in the box.

borrowed	budget	earn	expenses	lend	saved	student loan	taxes

1. Sandra doesn't have a lot of ________________ because she lives with her parents.
2. Alejandro talked to his father about his expenses and together they made a ________________.
3. You can apply for a ________________ through a bank or a government program.
4. Enrique ________________ money from his uncle last year.
5. Often, students who work don't have to pay ________________ because their income is low.
6. Can you ________________ me $20? I'll pay you back on Friday.
7. Rafael doesn't ________________ much money from his job.
8. Yua ________________ almost all of the money she earned from her job last summer.

B Circle the correct verb to complete each sentence.

1. Did you know the library has ebooks you can *borrow* / *lend*?
2. The library *borrows* / *lends* ebooks for 14 days.
3. Beatriz has a student loan. She *borrowed* / *lent* $2,500 from the bank.
4. The bank *borrows* / *lends* money to students at a low interest rate.
5. Hayato never needs to *borrow* / *lend* money because he follows a budget carefully.
6. Will your parents *borrow* / *lend* you money for college?
7. Mr. Rainha won't *borrow* / *lend* any more money to his son.
8. The bank *borrowed* / *lent* me some money and I *borrowed* / *lent* some from my parents.

C Match the *if* clause to the main clause.

______	**1.** If you live with your parents,	**a.** you pay interest.
______	**2.** If you borrow money,	**b.** it's cheaper.
______	**3.** If you save money in the bank,	**c.** make sure you pay it back on time.
______	**4.** If the bank lends money to you,	**d.** tell them to pay you back soon.
______	**5.** If you make coffee at home,	**e.** you have fewer expenses.
______	**6.** If someone borrows money from you,	**f.** you earn interest.

D 33 Listen to the sentences. Does each main clause talk about facts or give instructions? Circle *Fact* or *Instructions*.

1.	Fact	Instructions	**4.**	Fact	Instructions	**7.**	Fact	Instructions
2.	Fact	Instructions	**5.**	Fact	Instructions			
3.	Fact	Instructions	**6.**	Fact	Instructions			

Lesson B Listening

A 34 Listen and circle **T** for *true* or **F** for *false*.

1. Plastic is very useful.	T	F
2. Everybody knows how much plastic they use every day.	T	F
3. Things that are made of plastic last a long, long time.	T	F
4. Paint isn't *biodegradable*.	T	F
5. Things that are biodegradable hurt the environment.	T	F
6. Most plastic is biodegradable.	T	F
7. Wood isn't biodegradable.	T	F
8. People need to think about the way they use plastic more.	T	F

▲ Shells are biodegradable. Plastic bottles are not.

B 34 Listen again. Choose the correct answer to complete each sentence.

1. If something is biodegradable, _______.
a. it breaks down naturally **b.** it is made from plastic **c.** it hurts the environment

2. The sentence, *Every piece of plastic ever made still exists*, means _______.
a. plastic breaks down easily **b.** plastic is recyclable **c.** plastic doesn't break down

3. _______ is an example of something that is biodegradable.
a. A plastic toy **b.** A dead tree **c.** A plastic bottle

4. Things that are man-made are _______.
a. good for the environment **b.** biodegradable **c.** not natural

C Use the phrases to write sentences in the zero conditional.

1. If you want bottled water,	it's not bad for the environment.
2. If something is not natural,	don't use single-use plastic.
3. If people understand that plastic isn't biodegradable,	it's not biodegradable.
4. If something is biodegradable,	maybe they will change the way they use it.
5. If you have to use plastic,	get a reusable water bottle.
6. If you want to reduce plastic waste,	make sure you recycle it.

1. ________________________________

2. ________________________________

3. ________________________________

4. ________________________________

5. ________________________________

6. ________________________________

Lesson C Vocabulary and Grammar

A Circle the correct verb to complete each sentence.

1. How much cash do you *carry* / *find* in your wallet?
2. I can *borrow* / *lend* you some money. When can you pay it back?
3. Valeria lives in an expensive apartment. She *saves* / *spends* a lot on rent.
4. Did you ever *make* / *win* the lottery?
5. Someone *lost* / *stole* money from the cash register.
6. Is it a good idea to *carry* / *change* money at the airport?
7. Someone *found* / *lost* $20 and Esteban *found* / *lost* it.
8. I don't buy lottery tickets because I never *lose* / *win*.
9. Fumiko has a difficult job, but she *changes* / *makes* a lot of money.

B Match the *if* clause to the main clause.

_______ 1. If they borrow money from the bank,
_______ 2. If we lend you money,
_______ 3. If employees steal from the store,
_______ 4. If you don't buy lottery tickets,
_______ 5. If we travel to Japan,
_______ 6. If you spend too much money on clothes,

a. you'll never win.
b. you won't be able to pay your bills.
c. we'll need to change our dollars for yen.
d. we will fire them.
e. they'll pay interest on the loan.
f. will you spend it wisely?

C Fill in the verbs in the first conditional sentences.

1. If I (pay) _______________ in cash now, I (not get) _______________ a credit card bill later.
2. If you (buy) _______________ me a coffee today, I (buy) _______________ you one tomorrow.
3. If you (take) _______________ the bus, it (cost) _______________ less than a taxi.
4. If someone (steal) _______________ your wallet, you probably (not get) _______________ it back.
5. If Ernesto (work) _______________ hard, he (earn) _______________ a good income.
6. If you (pay) _______________ with cash, you (get) _______________ 10% off.
7. If she (wins) _______________ the money, what (do) _______________ she _______________ with it?
8. If you (not save) _______________ money, you (not be able to) _______________ buy a car.

D Find the error with the first conditional in each sentence. Change the sentence so it is correct.

1. If she asks you for money, you will give it to her?
2. You work in this country, you will have to pay taxes.
3. If she doesn't get a job, how does she pay her expenses?
4. If they can't get a loan, they not buy a new car.
5. You save $200 a month, if you'll have $2,400 at the end of the year.
6. If you will not graduate from college, what will you do?

Nature Vacations

As one of the world's biggest travel companies, we are always thinking of new and exciting ways to make travel fun and interesting. We are pleased to announce some exciting new adventure vacations that we hope will bring our customers closer to nature. They will all be open for reservations next year. Please read about these special new destinations below!

Featured Vacations...

Mountain Camp

People will walk to this camp, high in the beautiful mountains. About 30 people will stay in the camp, and every day they will go walking in small groups. Tour guides will teach them about the animals in the mountains. Guests will sleep in small buildings made from local trees, and they will carry all their garbage home with them.

Rainforest Hotel

The building will be very tall so that 200 guests can see the tops of the trees. A theater will show movies about the plants and animals of the rainforest. A restaurant will serve dishes made from rainforest plants, and a shop will sell rainforest products. People will fly to a new airport near the hotel, so we won't need roads through the rainforest.

Coral Reef Ship

About 500 people will be on this ship. Tour guides will take guests swimming on the coral reefs so they can see fish and beautiful coral. On the ship, there will be information about preserving the coral reefs, and scientists will teach classes about saving the environment. Guests can eat coral reef fish in the ship's restaurant.

A Which place is it? Circle all the correct answers.

1. Guests will learn about the environment.
   Rainforest Hotel | Coral Reef Ship | Mountain Camp
2. People will see fish.
   Rainforest Hotel | Coral Reef Ship | Mountain Camp
3. It will be large.
   Rainforest Hotel | Coral Reef Ship | Mountain Camp
4. Guests will go walking.
   Rainforest Hotel | Coral Reef Ship | Mountain Camp
5. People will eat local food from this place.
   Rainforest Hotel | Coral Reef Ship | Mountain Camp
6. People can buy gifts from this place.
   Rainforest Hotel | Coral Reef Ship | Mountain Camp

B Which of these places is the WORST for the environment? Explain your answer. Use sentences with *if*.

____

____

____

____

____

____

____

C Which of these places is the BEST for the environment? Explain your answer. Use sentences with *if*.

____

____

____

____

____

____

____

____

Lesson E Writing

A Read about Yuko's situation. Then complete the email with the linking words and phrases in the box.

Yuko is a student at a four-year university. She doesn't have enough money to pay for her final year. She has to make a decision between borrowing money or leaving school for one year to work to earn money for her final year.

and also	however	on the one hand	on the other hand	on the whole

Hi Yuko,

I'm glad that your classes are going well and you like school. But you have a difficult decision to make about next year. (1) ________________, getting a student loan makes sense. If you do that, you won't interrupt your studies and you won't miss your friends. (2) ________________, you'll have a loan that you have to pay back.

(3) ________________, if you leave school to work for a year, you will get some work experience. (4) ________________, if you have work experience, you will have something to put on your resume. So, (5) ________________, I think you should take a year off from school to work and earn money.

B Write the linking words and phrases in the correct column.

both	however	I think	in addition	in conclusion	in contrast
it also	on the one hand	on the other hand	on the whole	overall	similarly

Describing Similarities	Comparing Differences	Concluding

C Read about Carolina's situation. Then write a few sentences to help her make a decision. Use some of the linking words and phrases in **B** to compare and contrast.

Carolina was accepted to two universities. She is very excited, but she has to make a difficult decision. State University offered her a scholarship. If she goes to State University, she won't need to borrow money. Ivy University also accepted her, but didn't offer her a scholarship. If she goes to Ivy, she will need to get a loan. Both universities are good, but Carolina thinks Ivy is better. What should she do?

____

____

____

____

____

Review

A Complete the sentences with the correct words from the box.

borrow	budget	earn	expenses	income	lend	save	student loan

1. Families with children have a lot of ________________. They must pay for food, clothes, and education for their children.
2. You should make a ________________ to plan how to spend your money.
3. Can you ________________ me $10? I don't have enough money to buy lunch.
4. I want to buy a car. I'm going to ________________ some money every month.
5. She'll start to pay back her ________________ after she graduates.
6. Jason has a very good ________________. He's an actor, and he gets a lot of money from his movies.
7. Most people have to ________________ money when they want to buy a house.
8. Mauricio is looking for a part-time job because he needs to ________________ some money.

B Fill in the verbs in the first conditional sentences.

1. If I (eat) ________________ more vegetables, I (lose) ________________ weight.
2. If you (lend) ________________ money to Kimberly, you (not get) ________________ it back!
3. You (learn) ________________ a lot of new words if you (read) ________________ English magazines.
4. You (get) ________________ stronger if you (work out) ________________ at the gym every day.
5. If I (buy) ________________ a new cell phone, I (not have) ________________ money for my bills.
6. He (not be) ________________ able to buy a car if he (not save) ________________ money.

C Unscramble the words to make sentences. Remember to use a comma after the *if* clause.

1. she gets / she will save / if / money on rent / a roommate

   ____

2. to Berlin / if / they will look / they move / for new jobs

   ____

3. the trip / we take / if / will take / three hours / the high-speed train

   ____

4. I can't pay cash / my credit card / I'll have to use / if / for the taxi

   ____

5. any free time / if / this semester / you won't have / you take five classes

   ____

6. at the airport / a good exchange rate / if / we won't get / we change money

   ____

7. you use your credit card / you'll get / a better exchange rate / if

   ____

Video How to Buy Happiness

A Answer the questions.

1. What things do you like spending money on? For example, do you like going to restaurants, buying clothes, or buying gifts for other people? ______________________________

____

2. What things do you dislike spending money on? For example, do you dislike buying clothes or groceries? ______________________________

____

B Watch the video and read the sentences. Then circle **T** for *true* or **F** for *false*.

1. Michael Norton agrees that money can't buy happiness. T F
2. Norton wanted to compare what happens when people spend money on themselves and when people give money away. T F
3. Some students in each group bought coffee. T F
4. Every student was given $20. T F
5. The students who received less money were happier. T F
6. People who spent the money on someone else were happier. T F
7. The results in Canada were different from the results in Uganda. T F
8. Giving to charity can make people happier. T F

C Use the phrases to write sentences in the zero conditional.

1. If the students spend money on themselves,	they feel happier.
2. If the students spend money on others,	don't spend money on another product for yourself, spend it on someone else.
3. If someone gives money to charity,	they don't feel happier.
4. If you want to be happier,	it makes them happier.

1. ______________________________
2. ______________________________
3. ______________________________
4. ______________________________

D In your notebook, answer the questions.

1. If someone gave you $20 and said you had to spend it today on yourself, how would you spend it? Why?
2. If someone gave you $20 and said you had to spend it today on someone else, how would you spend it? Why?

Spelling Rules for Verbs Ending in -s and -es

1. Add *-s* to most verbs.	like-like**s** sit-sit**s**
2. Add *-es* to verbs that end in *-ch, -s, -sh, -x,* or *-z.*	catch-catch**es** miss-miss**es** wash-wash**es** mix-mix**es** buzz-buzz**es**
3. Change the *-y* to *-i* and add *-es* when the base form ends in a consonant + *-y.*	cry-cr**ies** carry-carr**ies**
4. Do not change the *-y* when the base form ends in a vowel + *-y.*	pay-pay**s** stay-stay**s**
5. Some verbs are irregular in the third-person singular *-s* form of the simple present.	be-**is** go-**goes** do-**does** have-**has**

Spelling Rules for Verbs Ending in *-ing*

1. Add *-ing* to the base form of most verbs.	eat-eat**ing** do-do**ing** speak-speak**ing** carry-carry**ing**
2. When the verb ends in a consonant + *-e*, drop the *-e* and add *-ing.*	ride-rid**ing** write-writ**ing**
3. For one-syllable verbs that end in a consonant + a vowel + a consonant (CVC), double the final consonant and add *-ing.*	stop-stop**ping** sit-sit**ting**
Do not double the final consonant for verbs that end in CVC when the final consonant is *-w, -x,* or *-y.*	show-show**ing** fix-fix**ing** stay-stay**ing**
4. For two-syllable verbs that end in CVC and have stress on the first syllable, add *-ing.* Do not double the final consonant.	ENter-enter**ing** LISTen-listen**ing**
For two-syllable verbs that end in CVC and have stress on the last syllable, double the final consonant and add *-ing.*	beGIN-begin**ning** ocCUR-occur**ring**

Spelling Rules for Verbs Ending in *-ed*

1. Add *-ed* to the base form of most verbs that end in a consonant.	start-start**ed** talk-talk**ed**
2. Add *-d* if the base form of the verb ends in *-e.*	dance-danc**ed** live-liv**ed**
3. When the base form of the verb ends in a consonant + *-y*, change the *-y* to *-i* and add *-ed.*	cry-cr**ied** worry-worr**ied**
Do not change the *-y* to *-i* when the verb ends in a vowel + *-y.*	stay-stay**ed**
4. For one-syllable verbs that end in a consonant + a vowel + a consonant (CVC), double the final consonant and add *-ed.*	stop-stop**ped** rob-rob**bed**
Do not double the final consonant of verbs that end in *-w, -x,* or *-y.*	follow-follow**ed** fix-fix**ed** play-play**ed**
5. For two-syllable verbs that end in CVC and have stress on the first syllable, add *-ed.* Do not double the final consonant.	ORder-order**ed** HAPpen-happen**ed**
For two-syllable verbs that end in CVC and have stress on the last syllable, double the final consonant and add *-ed.*	ocCUR-occur**red** preFER-prefer**red**

Spelling Rules for Comparative and Superlative Forms

	Adjective/ Adverb	Comparative	Superlative
1. Add *-er* or *-est* to one-syllable adjectives and adverbs.	tall fast	tall**er** fast**er**	tall**est** fast**est**
2. Add *-r* or *-st* to adjectives that end in *-e*.	nice	nice**r**	nice**st**
3. Change the *-y to -i* and add *-er* or *-est* to two-syllable adjectives and adverbs that end in *-y*.	easy happy	eas**ier** happ**ier**	eas**iest** the happ**iest**
4. Double the final consonant and add *-er* or *-est* to one-syllable adjectives or adverbs that end in a consonant + a vowel + a consonant (CVC).	big hot	big**ger** hot**ter**	big**gest** hot**test**

Common Irregular Verbs

Base Form	Simple Past	Past Participle	Base Form	Simple Past	Past Participle
begin	began	begun	make	made	made
break	broke	broken	meet	met	met
bring	brought	brought	pay	paid	paid
buy	bought	bought	put	put	put
come	came	come	read	read	read
do	did	done	ride	rode	ridden
drink	drank	drunk	run	ran	run
drive	drove	driven	say	said	said
eat	ate	eaten	see	saw	seen
feel	felt	felt	send	sent	sent
get	got	gotten	sit	sat	sat
give	gave	given	sleep	slept	slept
go	went	gone	speak	spoke	spoken
have	had	had	swim	swam	swum
hear	heard	heard	take	took	taken
hurt	hurt	hurt	tell	told	told
know	knew	known	think	thought	thought
leave	left	left	throw	threw	thrown
let	let	let	understand	understood	understood
lose	lost	lost	write	wrote	written

Phrasal Verbs (Separable) and Their Meanings		
*Don't forget to **turn off** the oven before you leave the house.* *Don't forget to **turn** the oven **off** before you leave the house.*		
Phrasal Verb	**Meaning**	**Example Sentence**
blow up	cause something to explode	*The workers **blew** the bridge **up**.*
bring back	return	*She **brought** the shirt **back** to the store.*
bring up	1. raise from childhood 2. introduce a topic to discuss	*1. My grandmother **brought** me **up**.* *2. Don't **bring up** that subject.*
call back	return a telephone call	*I **called** Rajil **back** but there was no answer.*
call off	cancel	*They **called** the wedding **off** after their fight.*
cheer up	make someone feel happier	*Her visit to the hospital **cheered** the patients **up**.*
clear up	clarify, explain	*She **cleared** the problem **up**.*
do over	do again	*His teacher asked him to **do** the essay **over**.*
figure out	solve, understand	*The student **figured** the problem **out**.*
fill in	complete information	***Fill in** the answers on the test.*
fill out	complete an application or form	*I had to **fill** many forms **out** at the doctor's office.*
find out	learn, uncover	*Did you **find** anything **out** about the new plans?*
give away	offer something freely	*They are **giving** prizes **away** at the store.*
give back	return	*The boy **gave** the pen **back** to the teacher.*
give up	stop doing	*I **gave up** sugar last year. Will you **give** it **up**?*
help out	aid, support someone	*I often **help** my older neighbors **out**.*
lay off	dismiss workers from their jobs	*My company **laid** 200 workers **off** last year.*
leave on	allow a machine to continue working	*I **left** the lights **on** all night.*
let in	allow someone to enter	*She opened a window to **let** some fresh air **in**.*
look over	examine	*We **looked** the contract **over** before signing it.*
make up	say something untrue or fictional (a story, a lie)	*The child **made** the story **up**. It wasn't true at all.*
pay back	return money, repay a loan	*I **paid** my friend **back**. I owed him $10.*
pick up	1. get someone or something 2. lift	*1. He **picked up** his date at her house.* *2. I **picked** the ball **up** and threw it.*
put off	delay, postpone	*Don't **put** your homework **off** until tomorrow.*
put out	1. take outside 2. extinguish	*1. He **put** the trash **out**.* *2. Firefighters **put out** the fire.*
set up	1. arrange 2. start something	*1. She **set** the tables **up** for the party.* *2. They **set up** the project.*
shut off	stop something from working	*Can you **shut** the water **off**?*
sort out	make sense of something	*We have to **sort** this problem **out**.*
straighten up	make neat and orderly	*I **straightened** the messy living room **up**.*
take back	own again	*He **took** the tools that he loaned me **back**.*
take off	remove	*She **took off** her hat and gloves.*
take out	remove	*I **take** the trash **out** on Mondays.*
talk over	discuss a topic until it is understood	*Let's **talk** this plan **ove**r before we do anything.*
think over	reflect, ponder	*She **thought** the job offer **over** carefully.*
throw away/ throw out	get rid of something, discard	*He **threw** the old newspapers **away**.* *I **threw out** the old milk in the fridge.*
try on	put on clothing to see if it fits	*He **tried** the shoes **on** but didn't buy them.*
turn down	refuse	*His manager **turned** his proposal **down**.*
turn off	stop something from working	*Can you **turn** the TV **off**, please?*
turn on	switch on, operate	*I **turned** the lights **on** in the dark room.*
turn up	increase the volume	***Turn** the radio **up**, so we can hear the news.*
wake up	make someone stop sleeping	*The noise **woke** the baby **up**.*
write down	write on paper	*I **wrote** the information **down**.*